Latin Primer 2
Student Edition

Latin Primer Series

Latin Primer: Book 1, Martha Wilson
Latin Primer 1: Student Edition
Latin Primer 1: Teacher's Edition
Latin Primer 1: Flashcard Set
Latin Primer 1: Audio Guide CD

Latin Primer: Book 2, Martha Wilson
Latin Primer 2: Student Edition
Latin Primer 2: Teacher's Edition
Latin Primer 2: Flashcard Set
Latin Primer 2: Audio Guide CD

Latin Primer: Book 3, Martha Wilson *(coming 2011)*
Latin Primer 3: Student Edition
Latin Primer 3: Teacher's Edition
Latin Primer 3: Flashcard Set
Latin Primer 3: Audio Guide CD

Published by Canon Press
P.O. Box 8729, Moscow, ID 83843
800.488.2034 | www.canonpress.com

Martha Wilson, *Latin Primer Book 2 Student Edition*
Copyright © 1993 by Martha Wilson.
Copyright © 2010 by Canon Press.
First Edition 1993, Second Edition 2003, Third Edition 2003,
Fourth Edition 2010

Cover design by Rachel Hoffmann.
Interior layout and design by Phaedrus Media.
Textual additions and edits by Laura Storm.
Printed in the United States of America.

All rights reserved. No part of this publication may be reproduced, stored in a retrieval system, or transmitted in any form by any means, electronic, mechanical, photocopy, recording, or otherwise, without prior permission of the author, except as provided by USA copyright law.

10 11 12 13 14 15 16   10 9 8 7 6 5 4 3 2 1

BOOK 2
Latin PRIMER

MARTHA WILSON / Edited by LAURA STORM

canonpress
Moscow, Idaho

Contents

Introduction vi
Pronunciation Guide vii

Unit 1: Weeks 1–8   2

Week 1: Review—First declension noun endings 5
Week 2: Review—Second declension noun endings 11
Week 3: Review—Second declension neuter noun endings 17
Week 4: Review—Present active verb endings 23
Week 5: Review—Future active verb endings 29
Week 6: Review—Imperfect active verb endings 35
Week 7: Review—General 41
Week 8: Review—General 47

Unit 2: Weeks 9–16   53

Week 9: Third conjugation verbs in the present tense, *dūcō* 55
Week 10: *Sum* review / Predicate adjectives and declining adjectives 61
Week 11: Third conjugation verbs in the future tense, *dūcam* 67
Week 12: Third conjugation verbs in the imperfect tense, *dūcēbam* ... 73
Week 13: Third declension noun endings 79
Week 14: Review—General 85
Week 15: Third declension neuter noun endings 91
Week 16: *Erō* (future of *sum*) / Predicate nouns 97

Unit 3: Weeks 17–24   103

Week 17: Accusative case and direct objects 105
Week 18: Accusative case, focus on neuter nouns 111
Week 19: Review—Accusative case / direct objects 117

Week 20: Review—Accusative case / direct objects 123
Week 21: Questions (*-ne*) 129
Week 22: Commands 135
Week 23: Fourth declension noun endings 141
Week 24: Review—General 147

Unit 4: Weeks 25–32 153

Week 25: Fourth declension neuter noun endings 155
Week 26: Review—Fourth declension noun endings 161
Week 27: *Possum* review / Infinitives 167
Week 28: Review—General 173
Week 29: Review—General 179
Week 30: *Eram* (imperfect of *sum*) 185
Week 31: Review—General 191
Week 32: Review—General 197

Appendices 205

Chant Charts 206
Glossary 214
Sources and Helps 223

INTRODUCTION

Welcome to the *Latin Primer 2!* You now have one year of Latin behind you—congratulations! Your main work last year was to memorize chants and learn vocabulary. All together you learned about four hundred words! This year, you'll notice that your Word Lists include not only new words, but old favorites as well. (And sometimes exercises will include old words you might not have seen since last year . . . just to keep you on your toes!)

Your main job this year is to begin to read and write more advanced Latin sentences. A large part of being able to read and write Latin is having lots of things (especially vocabulary!) tucked away in your memory, ready to use. By the end of this year you'll be able to translate sentences like, *Latrō quondam erat eques mīrus* ("The robber was once a wonderful knight") and *Lupī cervum nōn possunt oppugnāre* ("The wolves are not able to attack the deer").

As you learn more advanced Latin, you'll notice that you'll understand even better how our English language works. Since you're so used to using English, there are many things about it that you won't even notice until you see how Latin is different.

You may have realized last year that Latin appears in many places. I hope over the last year you've been able to recognize English names and other words that come from Latin. Maybe you've seen Latin on buildings, coins, or memorials. I've discovered that many colleges have Latin on their seals. You had a list of some of those in *Latin Primer 1,* and you'll be learning a couple more this year!

Once, at the end of a dinner I was having with my grandmother, she said with satisfaction, *"Fīnis."* Learning Latin may not be quite as easy as eating dinner, but I hope you'll be able to say *"fīnis"* with satisfaction at the end of this year. Instead of being full of meat and potatoes, you'll be full of new knowledge!

Valēte,
Martha Wilson

Pronunciation Guide

Vowels:

Vowels in Latin have only two pronunciations, long and short. When speaking, long vowels are held twice as long as short vowels. Long vowels are marked with a "macron" or line over the vowel (e.g., ā). Vowels without a macron are short vowels.

When spelling a word, including the macron is important, as it can determine the meaning of the word (e.g., liber is a noun meaning *book*, and līber is an adjective meaning *free*).

Long Vowels:
- ā like *a* in *father*: frāter, suprā
- ē like *e* in *obey*: trēs, rēgīna
- ī like *i* in *machine*: mīles, vīta
- ō like *o* in *holy*: sōl, glōria
- ū like *oo* in *rude*: flūmen, lūdus
- ȳ like *i* in *chip*: grȳps, cȳgnus

Short Vowels:
- a like *a* in *idea*: canis, mare
- e like *e* in *bet*: et, terra
- i like *i* in *this*: hic, silva
- o like *o* in *domain*: bonus, nomen
- u like *u* in *put*: sum, sub

Diphthongs:

A combination of two vowel sounds collapsed together into one syllable is a dipthong:

- ae like *ai* in *aisle*   caelum, saepe
- au like *ou* in *house*   laudo, nauta
- ei like *ei* in *reign*   deinde
- eu like *eu* in *eulogy*   Deus
- oe like *oi* in *oil*   moenia, poena
- ui like *ew* in *chewy*   huius, hui

Consonants:

Latin consonants are pronounced with the same sounds with the following exceptions:

- c   like *c* in *come*   never soft like *city*, *cinema*, or *peace*
- g   like *g* in *go*   never soft like *gem*, *geology*, or *gentle*
- v   like *w* in *wow*   never like *Vikings*, *victor*, or *vacation*
- s   like *s* in *sissy*   never like *easel*, *weasel*, or *peas*
- ch like *ch* in *chorus*   never like *church*, *chapel*, or *children*
- r   is trilled   like a dog snarling, or a machine gun
- i   like *y* in *yes*   when used before a vowel at the beginning of a word, between two vowels within a word, otherwise it's usually used as a vowel

Unit One

Unit 1: Goals

By the end of Week 8, you should be able to . . .

- Chant from memory the first declension, second declension, and second declension neuter noun endings
- Recognize and distinguish first declension, second declension, and second declension neuter nouns
- Decline any first declension, second declension, or second declension neuter noun
- Chant from memory the present, future, and imperfect verb ending chants
- Recognize and distinguish first and second conjugation verbs by their stems
- Translate simple present, future, and imperfect tense sentences (e.g., *Delphīnī properābant* means "The dolphins were rushing")

WEEK 1

Word List

NOUNS

1. amīcus, -ī (m) . . . . friend
2. aqua, -ae (f) . . . . water
3. caelum, -ī (n) . . . . sky, heaven
4. cibus, -ī (m) . . . . food
5. colōnus, -ī (m) . . . . . . settler
6. equus, -ī (m) . . . . horse
7. latebra, -ae (f) . . . . . . hiding place
8. mūrus, -ī (m) . . . . wall
9. nauta, -ae (m) . . . . . . sailor
10. nimbus, -ī (m) . . . . . thundercloud, storm
11. poēta, -ae (m) . . . . . poet
12. pontus, -ī (m) . . . . . . sea, seawater
13. puella, -ae (f) . . . . . . girl
14. puer, puerī (m) . . . . . boy
15. stella, -ae (f) . . . . . . star
16. taurus, -ī (m) . . . . . . bull
17. terra, -ae (f) . . . . earth, land
18. virga, -ae (f) . . . . branch, twig

VERBS

19. peccō, peccāre . . . . . I sin
20. astō, astāre . . . . I stand near, stand by

Chant:
First Declension Noun Endings

	LATIN			ENGLISH	
	SINGULAR	PLURAL		SINGULAR	PLURAL
NOMINATIVE	-a	-ae		a, the *noun*	the *nouns*
GENITIVE	-ae	-ārum		of the *noun*, the *noun's*	of the *nouns*, the *nouns'*
DATIVE	-ae	-īs		to, for the *noun*	to, for the *nouns*
ACCUSATIVE	-am	-ās		the *noun*	the *nouns*
ABLATIVE	-ā	-īs		by, with, from the *noun*	by, with, from the *nouns*

(Continued on the next page)

Latin Primer Book 2

> **Quotation:**
> *Amīcus verus est rara avis*—"A true friend is a rare bird"

WEEK 1 *Derivatives:* _____

_____
_____
_____
_____
_____
_____
_____
_____
_____
_____
_____
_____

Quotation: _____

_____
_____

Weekly Worksheet 1

name: _____

A. Cross out the two wrong words in the definition below and write the correct words above them. Then, using the lines below, list all the Latin nouns from this week's Word List, their genitive ending, and gender. The first one is done for you.

A noun describes a person, place, or action.

1. _____amīcus, -ī (m)_____   10. _____
2. _____   11. _____
3. _____   12. _____
4. _____   13. _____
5. _____   14. _____
6. _____   15. _____
7. _____   16. _____
8. _____   17. _____
9. _____   18. _____

B. Complete the review chant for this week and answer the questions about it.

	SINGULAR	PLURAL
	-a	
DATIVE		
ACCUSATIVE		
ABLATIVE		

1. Are these endings for nouns or verbs? _____

7

2. Which declension are these endings for? _____

3. What is the gender of most nouns in this declension? _____

4. Which ending tells you a noun's declension? _____

C. Decline *virga, -ae* in the chart below, then answer the questions.

	SINGULAR	PLURAL
NOM.	virga	
GEN.		
DAT.		
ACC.		
ABL.		

1. The word *virga* means _____.

2. Last year, you learned the word *virgō*, which means _____.

D. Use your knowledge of Latin to answer the following questions about derivatives. Remember, a derivative is an English word with a Latin root.

1. The English word *noun* comes from the Latin word *nomen*, which means _____.

2. An *aquarium* is like a zoo for sea animals. *Aquarium* is a derivative of the Latin word _____.

3. A *peccadillo* is small mistake. *Peccadillo* is a derivative of the Latin word _____.

Give an English derivative for each of these words.

4. mūrus _____

5. poēta _____

6. terra _____

7. equus _____

The word for "friend" in Latin is *amīcus*. Look at the word for "friend" in these languages.

ITALIAN	amico
SPANISH	amigo
FRENCH	ami

8. Why do they look so much like *amīcus*? _____

_____

_____

E. Complete the chart!

	ENGLISH: SINGULAR	LATIN: SINGULAR	LATIN: PLURAL
1.		nauta	
2.		puella	
3.	wall		
4.		latebra	
5.			pontī
6.	poet		
7.	horse		
8.			colōnī
9.		cibus	
10.	bull		

Latin Primer Book 2

F. For each noun, give its declension and gender. Then decline each noun by adding the endings to the base that is given. Each noun's nominative and genitive singular forms are provided.

DECLENSION _____ GENDER _____

	SINGULAR	PLURAL
NOM.	aqua	aqu
GEN.	aquae	aqu
DAT.	aqu	aqu
ACC.	aqu	aqu
ABL.	aqu	aqu

DECLENSION _____ GENDER _____

	SINGULAR	PLURAL
NOM.	latebra	latebr
GEN.	latebrae	latebr
DAT.	latebr	latebr
ACC.	latebr	latebr
ABL.	latebr	latebr

1. How do you find the base of a noun? _____
_____

G. Answer the questions about this week's quotation.

1. What does *Amīcus verus est rara avis* mean in English? _____
_____

2. Which Latin word is the subject of this quotation? _____

3. What case does the subject noun always take? _____

4. Which Latin word is the verb? (Hint: you should recognize it from last year!) _____

H. On the lines below, give the Latin word for each object.

1. _____   2. _____   3. _____

WEEK 2

Word List

NOUNS

1. ariēna, -ae (f) . . . . banana
2. cunīculus, -ī (m) . . . . . rabbit
3. folium, -ī (n) . . . . leaf
4. frāgum, -ī (n) . . . . . . strawberry
5. hortus, -ī (m) . . . . . . garden
6. mālum, -ī (n) . . . . apple
7. pirum, -ī (n) . . . . pear
8. ūva, -ae (f) . . . . grape

ADJECTIVES

9. aprīcus, -a, -um . . . . . . sunny
10. dēliciōsus, -a, -um . . . delicious
11. magnus, -a, -um . . . . . large, big
12. malus, -a, -um . . . . . . bad, evil
13. parvus, -a, -um . . . . . little, small

VERBS

14. gustō, gustāre . . . . . . I taste

Chant:

Second Declension Noun Endings

	LATIN		ENGLISH	
	SINGULAR	PLURAL	SINGULAR	PLURAL
NOM.	-us	-ī	a, the *noun*	the *nouns*
GEN.	-ī	-ōrum	of the *noun*, the *noun's*	of the *nouns*, the *nouns'*
DAT.	-ō	-īs	to, for the *noun*	to, for the *nouns*
ACC.	-um	-ōs	the *noun*	the *nouns*
ABL.	-ō	-īs	by, with, from the *noun*	by, with, from the *nouns*

 Quotation:
Magna Carta—"Great Charter"

WEEK 2 *Derivatives:*

Quotation:

Weekly Worksheet 2

name: _____

A. Complete the chant chart and answer the questions about it.

	SINGULAR	PLURAL
	-us	
DATIVE		
ABLATIVE		

1. Is this a noun ending or a verb ending chant? _____

2. Which declension is it? _____

3. Which gender are most of the nouns that take these endings? _____

B. Decline *hortus, -ī* in the chart below, then answer the questions about it.

	SINGULAR	PLURAL
NOM.		
GEN.		
DAT.		
ACC.		
ABL.		

1. Which ending tells you a noun's declension? _____

2. Which declension is *hortus*? _____

Latin Primer Book 2

3. What does *hortus* mean? _____

Decline *ariēna, -ae* in the chart below, then answer the questions about it.

	SINGULAR	PLURAL
NOM.	ariēna	
GEN.		
DAT.		
ACC.		
ABL.		

2. Which declension is *ariēna*? _____

3. What does *ariēna* mean? _____

C. For each noun, write in the blank whether it is in the first declension (1) or second declension (2).

1. cibus, -ī _____   5. pontus, -ī _____

2. stella, -ae _____   6. virga, -ae _____

3. cunīculus, -ī _____   7. poēta, -ae _____

4. aqua, -ae _____   8. puer, puerī _____

D. Translate these words into English. Can you do it from memory?

1. pirum _____   6. apricus _____

2. latebra _____   7. gustō _____

3. dēliciōsus _____   8. ūva _____

4. nimbus _____   9. astō _____

5. peccō _____   10. folium _____

E. Answer the questions about this week's quotation.

1. What does *Magna Carta* mean? _____

2. Who was king of England at the time the Magna Carta was written? _____

F. Write three sentences in English. In each sentence, replace two of the words with Latin words from this week. One sentence is given as an example.

1. <u>The *apple* is juicy and *delicious*.</u>   The *mālum* is juicy and *deliciosus*.

2. _____

3. _____

4. _____

G. Each sentence below uses a derivative (in italics). Use your knowledge of Latin vocabulary to finish each sentence by circling the correct answer!

1. If someone writes a *malicious* letter, she is being _____.

   a) funny   b) mean   c) thoughtful

2. "I'm going to go *apricate*" is just a fancy way to say "I'm going to go _____.

   a) lay in the sun   b) pick fruit   c) write a thank-you note

3. *Coney* Island got its name because hundreds of _____ used to live there.

   a) circus animals   b) poets   c) rabbits

4. *Horticulture* is the study of _____.

   a) how to raise toucans   b) how to grow plants   c) how to heal sicknesses

5. When a person is *magnanimous*, it means that he is _____.

   a) generous   b) afraid   c) short

WEEK 3

Word List

NOUNS

1. aedificium, -ī (n) . . . . . building
2. cēna, -ae (f) . . . . dinner, meal
3. dominus, -ī (m) . . . . . lord, master
4. epistula, -ae (f) . . . . . letter
5. fābula, -ae (f) . . . . . . story, legend
6. fēmina, -ae (f) . . . . . . woman
7. fīlia, -ae (f) . . . . daughter
8. fīlius, -ī (m) . . . . son
9. forum, -ī (n) . . . . public square, marketplace
10. lingua, -ae (f) . . . . . . tongue, language
11. mensa, -ae (f) . . . . . . table
12. porta, -ae (f) . . . . door, gate
13. sella, -ae (f) . . . . seat, chair
14. turba, -ae (f) . . . . crowd, mob

VERBS

15. ambulō, ambulāre . . . I walk
16. amō, amāre . . . . I love
17. exsultō, exsultāre . . . I leap up, dance, rejoice
18. laudō, laudāre . . . . . . I praise
19. occultō, occultāre . . . . I hide, conceal
20. probō, probāre . . . . . I approve

Chant:
Second Declension Neuter Noun Endings

	LATIN		ENGLISH	
	SINGULAR	PLURAL	SINGULAR	PLURAL
NOM.	-um	-a	a, the *noun*	the *nouns*
GEN.	-ī	-ōrum	of the *noun*, the *noun's*	of the *nouns*, the *nouns'*
DAT.	-ō	-īs	to, for the *noun*	to, for the *nouns*
ACC.	-um	-a	the *noun*	the *nouns*
ABL.	-ō	-īs	by, with, from the *noun*	by, with, from the *nouns*

(Continued on the next page)

Latin Primer Book 2

> **Quotation:**
> *Dominus tecum*—"May the Lord be with you"

WEEK 3 *Derivatives:* _____

_____

_____

_____

_____

_____

_____

_____

_____

_____

_____

_____

_____

Quotation: _____

_____

_____

Weekly Worksheet 3

name: _____

A. On the lines below, give the Latin word for each fruit.

1. _____ 2. _____ 3. _____

B. Write the delensions in the blanks, then complete the chants.

_____ DECLENSION

	SINGULAR	PLURAL
NOM.		
GEN.	-ae	
DAT.	-ae	
ACC.		
ABL.		

_____ DECLENSION

SINGULAR	PLURAL
	-ī
-ī	

_____ DECLENSION NEUTER

SINGULAR	PLURAL
-um	
-um	

Now, sort the nouns from this week's Word List and put them in the proper columns below. The first one is done for you.

1st DECLENSION	2nd DECLENSION	2nd DECLENSION NEUTER
		aedificium

C. Decline the following nouns and answer the questions about them.

Decline *aedificium, -ī.*

	SINGULAR	PLURAL
NOM.	aedificium	
GEN.		
DAT.		
ACC.		
ABL.		

1. What is the *genitive singular* ending of all second declension nouns?

    a) -us   b) -ae   c) -ī

2. What is the *nominative singular* ending of all second declension neuter nouns?

    a) -um   b) -us   c) -ī

3. Which declension is *aedificium* in?

    a) second declension neuter   b) first declension   c) second conjugation

Decline *lingua, -ae.*

	SINGULAR	PLURAL
NOM.	lingua	
GEN.		
DAT.		
ACC.		
ABL.		

4. What is the *genitive singular* ending of all first declension nouns?

   a) -a   b) -ae   c) -ī

5. What is the gender of most first declension nouns?

   a) feminine   b) masculine   c) neuter

Decline *fīlius, -ī*.

	SINGULAR	PLURAL
NOM.	fīlius	
GEN.		
DAT.		
ACC.		
ABL.		

6. What part of speech is *fīlius*?

   a) verb   b) adjective   c) noun

D. Fill in the blank with each noun's genitive singular ending. Then underline the correct definition for each word.

NOUN	GENITIVE	DEFINITION		
1. lingua	_____	wheel	language	house
2. forum	_____	door	stone	marketplace
3. dominus	_____	stream	lord	walkway
4. fābula	_____	dress	shoe	story
5. epistula	_____	letter	tree	picture
6. pirum	_____	grape	rabbit	pear

LATIN PRIMER BOOK 2

E. Answer the following questions about derivatives from this week's Word List. The derivatives are italicized.

1. The English word *bilingual* comes from the Latin word _____.

2. If someone is *bilingual* he can speak two _____.

3. The English word *epistle* comes from the Latin word _____.

4. The *epistles* of Paul are _____ written to different churches.

List one derivative for each of these words.

5. fābula _____   6. probō _____

F. Give each noun's declension and gender. Then decline it by adding the endings to the base that is given. Each noun's nominative and genitive singular forms are provided.

DECLENSION _____ GENDER _____

	SINGULAR	PLURAL
NOM.	cēna	cēn
GEN.	cēnae	cēn
DAT.	cēn	cēn
ACC.	cēn	cēn
ABL.	cēn	cēn

DECLENSION _____ GENDER _____

	SINGULAR	PLURAL
NOM.	pirum	pir
GEN.	pirī	pir
DAT.	pir	pir
ACC.	pir	pir
ABL.	pir	pir

1. How do you find the base of a noun? _____

_____

G. Translate these words from English into Latin. (Hint: Watch whether they're singular or plural!)

1. doors _____   4. buildings _____

2. masters _____   5. apple _____

3. sailor _____   6. sea _____

WEEK 4

Word List

NOUNS

1. coquus, -ī (m) . . . . cook, chef
2. fungus, -ī (m) . . . . mushroom, fungus
3. nasus, -ī (m) . . . . nose
4. nucleus, -ī (m) . . . . nut, kernel
5. porcus, -ī (m) . . . . pig
6. radius, -ī (m) . . . . staff, rod
7. silva, -ae (f) . . . . forest
8. ulmus, -ī (m) . . . . elm tree

ADJECTIVES

9. brūnus, -a, -um . . . . . . brown

10. odōrātus, -a, -um . . . . sweet-smelling, fragrant
11. perfectus, -a, um . . . . perfect

VERBS

12. cumulō, cumulāre . . . I pile up, fill up
13. olefactō, olefactāre . . I smell, sniff

ADVERBS

14. sub . . . . below, under
15. suprā . . . . above

Chant:
Present Active Verb Endings

LATIN			ENGLISH	
	SINGULAR	PLURAL	SINGULAR	PLURAL
1ST	-ō	-mus	I am *verbing*	we are *verbing*
2ND	-s	-tis	you are *verbing*	you all are *verbing*
3RD	-t	-nt	he/she/it is *verbing*	they are *verbing*

 ### Quotation:
Porcī parvī trēs—"the three little pigs"

WEEK 4 *Derivatives:*

Quotation:

Weekly Worksheet 4

name: _____

A. Answer the following questions about the verbs from this week's Word List.

1. A verb shows _____ or state of being.

2. How do you find a verb's stem? _____

_____

3. What is the stem of *olefactō*? _____

4. What is the stem of *cumulō*? _____

5. Are these "ā" family or "ē" family verbs? _____

6. Which conjugation are these verbs in? _____

B. Conjugate *cumulō* in the present tense and translate it.

LATIN   ENGLISH

	SINGULAR	PLURAL		SINGULAR	PLURAL
1ST	cumulō			I pile up	
2ND					
3RD					

C. Latin's present tense can be translated into English in three different ways. For example, *olefactō* can be translated "I smell," "I do smell," or "I am smelling." Using *olefactō* as an example, write three translations for each verb.

1. cumulō _____

2. gustō _____

3. probant _____

4. peccāmus _____

Latin Primer Book 2

5. laudās _____

6. astat _____

7. ambulātis _____

D. Underline the noun that goes with the verb and then translate the sentences.

NOUN	VERB	TRANSLATION
1. Porcus / Porcī	olefactant.	_____
2. Puella / Puellae	gustat.	_____
3. Cunīculus / Cunīculī	occultant.	_____
4. Nauta / Nautae	astant.	_____
5. Coquus / Coquī	exsultat.	_____

E. Each of the words below comes from a Latin root! Figure out which of your Latin words is the root, and then give its English meaning. The first one is done for you.

	ITALIAN	SPANISH	FRENCH	LATIN	ENGLISH
1.	fragola	fresa	fraise	frāgum	strawberry
2.	perfetto	perfecto	parfait		
3.	terra	tierra	terre		
4.	lingua	lengua	langue		
5.	naso	nariz	nez		

F. Underline the ending for each verb and translate it.

1. gustātis _____

2. olefactāmus _____

3. laudō _____

4. astās _____

5. peccat _____

6. ambulātis _____

G. Give the following forms of *silva*.

1. nominative singular _____

2. genitive singular _____

3. nominative plural _____

Give these forms of *nucleus*.

4. genitive singular _____

5. nominative plural _____

H. For each English word, circle the nominative plural in Latin.

	ENGLISH	LATIN		
1.	walls	mūra	mūrae	mūrī (m)
2.	elm trees	ulmus	ulmī	ulmōs (m)
3.	chairs	sellās	sellae	sella (f)
4.	seas	pontae	pontuses	pontī (m)
5.	letters	epistulae	epistula	epistulī (f)
6.	kernels	nucleuī	nucleī	nucleum (m)
7.	friends	amicī	amicae	amica (m)
8.	pears	pira	pirī	pirum (n)
9.	sons	fīlius	fīlium	fīliī (m)
10.	forests	silva	silvae	silvī (f)

I. Translate these Latin sentences into English. See if you can remember how to translate the last one!

1. Fīlia ambulat. _____

2. Turba exsultat. _____

3. Dominus amat. _____

4. Nasī olefactant. _____

5. Fēminae probant. _____

6. Puer occultat. _____

7. Amīcī ambulant. _____

8. Fīliī exsultant. _____

9. Fēmina cumulat. _____

10. Poēta gustābit. _____

J. Answer the questions about this week's quotation.

1. How would you say "the three little pigs" in Latin? _____

2. Which word means "three"? _____

3. Which declension is the Latin word for "pigs"? _____

K. The chart below is missing its labels! Fill in the blanks, then decline *sella*.

WEEK 5

Word List

NOUNS

1. agricola, -ae (m) . . . . . farmer
2. aquila, -ae (m/f) . . . . . eagle
3. armentum, -ī (n) . . . . . herd
4. cervus, -ī (m) . . . . stag, deer
5. coma, -ae (f) . . . . hair, leaves, wool, mane
6. lūna, -ae (f) . . . . moon
7. lupus, -ī (m) . . . . wolf
8. nuntius, -ī (m) . . . . . . message, messenger
9. rīpa, -ae (f) . . . . riverbank
10. saxum, -ī (n) . . . . rock

VERBS

11. appāreō, appārēre . . . I appear
12. clāmō, clāmāre . . . . . I shout
13. errō, errāre . . . . I wander
14. labōrō, labōrāre . . . . . I work, toil
15. lībō, lībāre . . . . I sip, taste
16. lūceō, lūcēre . . . . I shine, am bright
17. properō, properāre . . . I hurry, rush
18. spīrō, spīrāre . . . . I breathe
19. ululō, ululāre . . . . I howl, scream
20. volō, volāre . . . . I fly

Chant:
Future Active Verb Endings

	LATIN			ENGLISH	
	SINGULAR	PLURAL		SINGULAR	PLURAL
1ST	-bō	-bimus		I will *verb*	we will *verb*
2ND	-bis	-bitis		you will *verb*	you all will *verb*
3RD	-bit	-bunt		he/she/it will *verb*	they will *verb*

Quotation:
Auribus teneō lupum—"I hold a wolf by the ears"

WEEK 5 *Derivatives:*

Quotation:

Weekly Worksheet 5

name: _____

A. Fill in the blank with each verb's stem.

1. clāmō, clāmāre clā_____

2. spīrō, spīrāre _____

3. appāreō, appārēre _____

4. ululō, ululāre _____

5. lībō, lībāre _____

B. Answer the following questions about the verb *lūceō*.

1. What is the stem of *lūceō, lūcēre*? _____

2. Which verb family is *lūceō* in? _____

3. Which conjugation is it in? _____

Fill in the future tense endings. Then conjugate *lūceō* in the future tense and translate it.

	SINGULAR	PLURAL
1ST	-bō	
2ND		
3RD		

LATIN		ENGLISH	
SINGULAR	PLURAL	SINGULAR	PLURAL
1ST			
2ND			
3RD			

C. Give the English meaning of these Latin quotations.

1. Auribus teneō lupum _____

2. Dominus vōbīscum _____

3. Amīcus verus est rara avis _____

4. Magna Carta _____

5. Porcī parvī trēs _____

D. Underline the ending of each verb. Then translate the verb and state whether it is first, second, or third person. The first one is done for you!

	VERB	TRANSLATION	PERSON
1.	errā<u>mus</u>	we are wandering	first
2.	properat		
3.	ululābitis		
4.	lībō		
5.	volant		
6.	spīrābis		

E. Translate these Latin sentences into English.

1. Coma lūcet. _____

2. Cervī properābunt. _____

3. Dominus probat. _____

4. Lupī ululant. _____

5. Armentum errābit. _____

6. Porcī cumulābunt. _____

7. Nuntius clamat. _____

8. Nautae astant. _____

9. Fēmina peccat. _____

10. Poēta probābit. _____

F. Here are some interesting English words derived from this week's Word List! Look them up in an English dictionary and write their definitions on the lines. In the parentheses next to each word, write the Latin word it comes from.

1. aquiline: _____

_____ (_____)

2. lupine: _____

_____ (_____)

3. libation: _____

_____ (_____)

4. translucent: _____

_____ (_____)

5. spiracle: _____

_____ (_____)

G. Answer the following questions about nouns.

1. What is the definition of a noun? _____

_____

2. What case does a Latin subject noun take?_____

3. Find and circle all the nouns below!

cēna	exsultō	lingua	apricus	fungus
malus	perfectus	folium	volō	puer
dominus	radius	ariēna	odōrātus	suprā
ambulō	brūnus	latebra	nucleus	amō
mūrus	agricola	virga	nasus	cervus

H. First, label the noun cases in the gray boxes to the left, then decline *saxum, -ī*.

	SINGULAR	PLURAL

I. Give the Latin plural, gender (M, F, or N), declension (1 or 2), and singular translation of each noun.

	NOUN	PLURAL	GENDER	DECLENSION	TRANSLATION
1.	nauta, -ae				
2.	caelum, -ī				
3.	cibus, -ī				
4.	poēta, -ae				
5.	amīcus, -ī				

WEEK 6

Word List

NOUNS

1. alga, -ae (f) . . . . seaweed
2. bālaena, -ae (f) . . . . . . whale
3. delphīnus, -ī (m) . . . . . dolphin
4. fuscina, -ae (f) . . . . . . harpoon, trident
5. harēna, -ae (f) . . . . . . sand
6. hydrus, -ī (m) . . . . sea serpent
7. nausea, -ae (f) . . . . . . nausea, seasickness
8. ōceanus, -ī (m) . . . . . . ocean

ADJECTIVES

9. aequus, -a, -um . . . . . . level, even, calm
10. albus, -a, -um . . . . . . white
11. āridus, -a, -um . . . . . . dry
12. salsus, -a, -um . . . . . . salty, witty
13. ūmidus, -a, -um . . . . . wet

CONJUNCTIONS

14. et . . . . and

VERBS

15. instō, instāre . . . . I pursue eagerly, follow closely
16. rīdeō, rīdēre . . . . I laugh

ADVERBS

17. statim . . . . immediately

Chant:
Imperfect Active Verb Endings

LATIN			ENGLISH	
	SINGULAR	PLURAL	SINGULAR	PLURAL
1ST	-bam	-bāmus	I was *verbing*	we were *verbing*
2ND	-bās	-bātis	you were *verbing*	you all were *verbing*
3RD	-bat	-bant	he/she/it was *verbing*	they were *verbing*

(Continued on the next page)

Latin Primer Book 2

> **Quotation:**
> *ad nauseam*—"to the point of sickness"

WEEK 6 *Derivatives:* _____

_____

Quotation: _____

Weekly Worksheet 6 name:

A. Fill in the imperfect tense endings. Then conjugate *rīdeō* in the imperfect tense and translate it.

	SINGULAR	PLURAL
1ST	-bam	
2ND		
3RD		

LATIN

	SINGULAR	PLURAL
1ST		
2ND		
3RD		

ENGLISH

	SINGULAR	PLURAL
1ST		
2ND		
3RD		

Answer the following questions about this week's verbs.

1. What conjugation is *rīdeō*? _____

2. What conjugation is *instō*? _____

3. What is the stem of *instō*? _____

B. Translate the following sentences into English. Watch out—a few include adjectives! Do you remember how to translate using them?

1. Delphīnī exsultant et rīdent. _____

2. Bālaena alba appāret. _____

3. Nautae clāmant. _____

4. Fuscinae volābunt! _____

5. Statim occultat. _____

6. Ōceanus salus lūcet. _____

C. For each verb, first underline its ending. Then fill in the blanks to tell whether it's first, second, or third person and whether it's singular or plural. Finally, translate the verb into English. The first one is done for you.

	VERB	PERSON	NUMBER	TRANSLATION
1.	ulula<u>t</u>	3rd	singular	he/she/it howls
2.	instās			
3.	spirāmus			
4.	appārētis			
5.	properābis			
6.	lūcent			
7.	clamābō			
8.	volābant			

D. Draw a line to match each derivative with its Latin root.

1. humidifier   albus

2. baleen   spīrō

3. apparition   aequus

4. ridicule   rīdeō

5. albino   ūmidus

6. equator   appāreō

7. conspiracy   bālaena

E. For each sentence, underline the Latin noun and verb that match the English sentence.

ENGLISH	NOUN	VERB
1. A sea serpent is hiding.	Hydrus / Hydrī	occultat / occultātis.
2. The cooks were laughing.	Coquus / Coquī	rīdēbās / rīdēbunt / rīdēbant.
3. The herd hurries.	Armentum / Armenta	properat / properant.
4. The dolphins will follow closely.	Delphīnus / Delphīnī	instābant / instābunt / instant.
5. The rabbit was dancing.	Cunīculus / Cunīculī	exsultābam / exsultābat.

F. Decline the following nouns and write which declension each one is in. Then answer the questions.

_____ DECLENSION

	SINGULAR	PLURAL
NOM.	harēna	
GEN.		
DAT.		
ACC.		
ABL.		

_____ DECLENSION

	SINGULAR	PLURAL
NOM.	cibus	
GEN.		
DAT.		
ACC.		
ABL.		

1. Which case is used for subjects? _____

2. What is the gender of *cibus*? _____

3. What is the gender of *harēna*? _____

G. Answer the following questions about this week's quotation.

1. If you talk on and on and on about something, you are talking _____ .

2. What does that phrase mean in English? _____

H. Give the genitive singular ending of each noun, then write whether it is first declension (1), second declension (2), or second declension neuter (2N). The first one is done for you.

1. fuscina _____-ae___1_____   6. fungus _____

2. radius _____   7. rīpa _____

3. pontus _____   8. ulmus _____

4. alga _____   9. pirum _____

5. aedificium _____ 10. cēna _____

I. Find and circle the hidden vocabulary words!

statim	albus	odoratus	latebra	pecco
hortus	gusto	supra	puella	aequus
salsus	turba	ululo	mensa	deliciosus

```
l a t e b r a p u m i l t a
r e o m g a o m h o r t u s
e q i s r o i e c t m s r m
w u g u s t o h l a e i b x
v u i p b r a i y w n o a y
u s z r s p e c c o s n t e
o k w a m u s l i r a a a n
s m p a u s t a t i m i l a
a q u p a w r t a c h i b p
l x e u s h a u l u l o u h
s d l l c a b l u s i f s r
u u l a d e l i c i o s u s
s a a n o d o r a t u s i c
```

WEEK 7

Word List

NOUNS

1. inimīcus, -ī (m) . . . . . . personal enemy
2. morbus, -ī (m) . . . . . . sickness, disease
3. opera, -ae (f) . . . . . . effort, services
4. pharetra, -ae (f) . . . . . . quiver
5. sagitta, -ae (f) . . . . . . arrow
6. venēnum, -ī (n) . . . . . . poison
7. ventus, -ī (m) . . . . wind

VERBS

8. augeō, augēre . . . . . . I increase
9. censeō, censēre . . . . . I estimate
10. cibō, cibāre . . . . I feed
11. exanimō, exanimāre . . I kill
12. oppugnō, oppugnāre . I attack
13. parō, parāre . . . . I prepare
14. pugnō, pugnāre . . . . I fight
15. significō, significāre . . I indicate, point out
16. superō, superāre . . . . I defeat, conquer

Chant:

No new chant this week.

Quotation:

Sī ēsurierit inimīcus tuus, ciba illum.

"If your enemy is hungry, give him bread to eat." [Prov. 25:21a]

Latin Primer Book 2

WEEK 7 *Derivatives:* _____

_____

_____

_____

_____

_____

_____

_____

_____

Quotation: _____

_____

_____

Weekly Worksheet 7

name: _____

A. Write the nominative plural of these nouns from this week's Word List.

1. morbus _____   4. opera _____

2. sagitta _____   5. venēnum _____

3. pharetra _____   6. inimīcus _____

B. Answer the questions, then conjugate *pugnō* in the present, future, and imperfect tenses and translate it.

1. What is the stem of *pugnō*? _____

2. Which conjugation is *pugnō*? _____

Present Active

LATIN

	SINGULAR	PLURAL
1ST		
2ND		
3RD		

ENGLISH

	SINGULAR	PLURAL
1ST		
2ND		
3RD		

Future Active

LATIN

	SINGULAR	PLURAL
1ST		
2ND		
3RD		

ENGLISH

	SINGULAR	PLURAL
1ST		
2ND		
3RD		

LATIN PRIMER BOOK 2

Imperfect Active

	LATIN			ENGLISH	
	SINGULAR	PLURAL		SINGULAR	PLURAL
1ST					
2ND					
3RD					

C. For each sentence, underline the Latin noun and verb that match the English sentence.

ENGLISH	NOUN	VERB
1. The farmers estimate.	Agricola / Agricolae	censet / censent.
2. The enemies are increasing.	Inimīcus / Inimīcī	auget / augent.
3. An arrow flies.	Sagitta / Sagittae	volat / volant.
4. The stags will fight.	Cervus / Cervī	pugnat / pugnābatis / pugnābunt.
5. An eagle was hiding.	Aquila / Aquilae	occultābam / occultābat / occultābit.

D. On the lines below, label what each animal is called in Latin.

1. _____ 2. _____ 3. _____

4. _____ 5. _____ 6. _____

E. For each verb, first underline its ending. Then fill in the blanks to tell whether it's first, second, or third person and whether it's singular or plural. Finally, translate the verb into English. The first one is done for you.

	VERB	PERSON	NUMBER	TRANSLATION
1.	parant	3rd	plural	they prepare
2.	lūcētis			
3.	spīrat			
4.	significābimus			
5.	superant			
6.	censeō			
7.	cibābam			
8.	augēbitis			

F. In some of these sentences, the noun and verb don't match in number. Cross out the incorrect sentences and translate the rest.

1. Nimbī apparent. _____

2. Agricolae significābat. _____

3. Cervus properat. _____

4. Venēna exanimābunt. _____

5. Lūpus ululant. _____

G. Fill in the blanks to complete these Latin quotations.

1. ad _____

2. Auribus teneō _____

3. _____ ēsurierit _____ tuus, _____ illum.

H. Each of these verbs is in the present tense. Translate each one in three different ways.

1. censent _____

2. augēs _____

3. significāmus _____

4. parō _____

I. List the verbs from this week on the blank lines below, then circle the verbs in the second conjugation, or "ē" family. When you have finished, answer the questions below.

1. _____   6. _____

2. _____   7. _____

3. _____   8. _____

4. _____   9. _____

5. _____

10. The uncircled verbs are in the _____ conjugation.

11. Another name for these verbs is the "_____" family.

J. Each of the words below comes from a Latin root! Figure out which of your Latin words is the root, and then give its English meaning.

	ITALIAN	SPANISH	FRENCH	LATIN	ENGLISH
1.	lupo	lobo	loup		
2.	vento	viento	vent		
3.	balena	ballena	baleine		
4.	luna	luna	lune		

WEEK 8

Word List

NOUNS

1. noctua, -ae (f) . . . . owl
2. sciūrus, -ī (m) . . . . squirrel

VERBS

3. audeō, audēre . . . . . . I dare
4. occupō, occupāre . . . . I seize
5. valeō, valēre . . . . I am well
6. maneō, manēre . . . . . I remain, stay

Chant:

No new chant this week.

Quotation:

No quotation this week.

WEEK 8 *Derivatives:*

Weekly Worksheet 8

name: _____

A. The verbs below are all _____ person verbs. After each verb, write the subject and whether it is singular or plural. The first one is done for you.

VERB	SUBJECT	SINGULAR/PLURAL
1. libant	they	plural
2. properābant		
3. occupant		
4. exanimābit		
5. censet		
6. oppugnābunt		
7. audēt		

B. Use each of the verbs above to write your own Latin sentences! Match a noun with each verb. Remember, the noun needs to match the verb in number (singular/plural). Then translate your sentences into English.

1. _____
2. _____
3. _____
4. _____
5. _____
6. _____
7. _____

Latin Primer Book 2

C. Conjugate *valeō* and *occupō* in the present tense. Above each box, write the verb's conjugation.

_____ CONJUGATION

	SINGULAR	PLURAL
1ST		
2ND		
3RD		

_____ CONJUGATION

	SINGULAR	PLURAL

D. These sentences change a little at a time. See how quickly and accurately you can translate them.

1. Parō. _____

2. Parāmus. _____

3. Parat. _____

4. Agricola parat. _____

5. Agricolae parant. _____

6. Inimīcī parant. _____

7. Inimīcī oppugnant. _____

8. Inimīcus clamat. _____

9. Nuntius clamat. _____

10. Nuntius properat. _____

11. Lūpus properat. _____

12. Lūpī ululant. _____

13. Lūpī augent. _____

14. Armenta augent. _____

15. Armentum errat. _____

16. Noctua errat. _____

17. Noctua volat. _____

18. Sagitta volat. _____

19. Sagittae volant. _____

20. Sagitta apparet. _____

21. Lūna apparet. _____

22. Lūna lūcet. _____

23. Saxum lucet. _____

24. Saxa manent. _____

25. Cervi manent. _____

E. Decline *sciūrus,* and then answer the questions about it.

	SINGULAR	PLURAL
NOM.		
GEN.		
DAT.		
ACC.		
ABL.		

Circle the answer.

1. What is the *genitive singular* ending of all second declension nouns?

   a) -us   b) -īs   c) -ī

2. Which case does a subject noun always take?

   a) nominative   b) neuter   c) plural

3. What is the gender of *sciūrus*?

   a) neuter   b) feminine   c) masculine

F. Give a definition for these parts of speech.

1. Noun: _____

2. Verb: _____

G. Draw a line to match each derivative with its Latin root.

1. audacious	labōrō
2. valedictorian	occupō
3. clamor	audeō
4. occupation	lūna
5. belabor	lūceō
6. cervine	amō
7. horticulture	hortus
8. translucent	clāmō
9. amateur	valeō
10. lunar	cervus

Unit Two

LATIN PRIMER BOOK 2

UNIT 2: GOALS

By the end of Week 16, you should be able to . . .

- Recognize and conjugate third conjugation verbs in the present, future, and imperfect tenses
- Decline adjectives in their masculine, feminine, and neuter forms
- Recognize and translate predicate adjectives and predicate nouns
- Recognize and decline third declension nouns
- Conjugate *sum* in the present and future tenses

WEEK 9

Word List

NOUNS

1. āla, -ae (f) . . . . wing
2. ancora, -ae (f) . . . . anchor
3. astrum, -ī (n) . . . . star, constellation
4. aurōra, -ae (f) . . . . dawn
5. fluvius, -ī (m) . . . . river, stream
6. prōra, -ae (f) . . . . prow (of a ship)
7. rēmus, -ī (m) . . . . oar
8. unda, -ae (f) . . . . wave
9. vēlum, -ī (n) . . . . sail, curtain

ADJECTIVES

10. aliēnus, -a, -um . . . . . foreign
11. aptus, -a, -um . . . . . . suitable, fit, ready
12. gelidus, -a, -um . . . . . cold, icy
13. lātus, -a, -um . . . . wide, broad
14. mīrus, -a, -um . . . . . . strange, wonderful
15. serēnus, -a, -um . . . . . calm, bright, clear

VERBS

16. dūcō, dūcere . . . . I lead
17. hiemō, hiemāre . . . . . I spend the winter
18. nāvigō, nāvigāre . . . . I sail
19. spectō, spectāre . . . . I look at, watch

Chant:

Dūcō, *I lead*—Present Active
Third Conjugation or "e" Family Verb

LATIN

	SINGULAR	PLURAL
1ST	dūcō	dūcimus
2ND	dūcis	dūcitis
3RD	dūcit	dūcunt

ENGLISH

	SINGULAR	PLURAL
1ST	I lead	we lead
2ND	you lead	you all lead
3RD	he/she/it leads	they lead

Quotation:

Ālīs volat propriīs—"She flies on her own wings"
(Motto for the state of Oregon)

WEEK 9 *Derivatives:*

Quotation:

Weekly Worksheet 9

name:

A. Conjugate and translate this week's verb chant, then answer the questions about it.

LATIN

	SINGULAR	PLURAL
1ST	dūcō	
2ND		
3RD		

ENGLISH

	SINGULAR	PLURAL
1ST	I lead	
2ND		
3RD		

1. Which conjugation is *dūcō, dūcere* in? _____

2. Which family is it in? _____

3. How do you find the stem of *dūcō* and other verbs in this conjugation? _____

_____

4. Do verbs in this conjugation act just like the other conjugations you've learned? _____

B. Below is a list of *singular* adjectives. As you learned last year, adjectives can have masculine, feminine, or neuter endings. Decide which ending each adjective has, and then write in the blank M (masculine), F (feminine), or N (neuter).

1. serēnus _____   4. mīrum _____   7. apta _____

2. aliēna _____   5. gelidum _____   8. lātus _____

All of these adjectives are *plural*. Like you did above, fill in the blank with whether they are M (masculine), F (feminine), or N (neuter).

10. aliēna _____   13. mīra _____   16. lātī _____

11. aptae _____   14. gelidī _____   17. serēnae _____

C. Fill in the blanks.

1. An adjective describes a _____ or a _____.

Latin Primer Book 2

2. In Latin, adjectives must match the _____ they describe in _____, _____, and _____.

D. Below are noun and adjective phrases in Latin. For each phrase, underline the noun's ending and circle the adjective's ending. Then translate each phrase. (Hint: The last two phrases are plural.)

1. āla lāta _____

2. fluvius lātus _____

3. aurōra gelida _____

4. vēlum mīrum _____

5. harēna serēna _____

6. astra aliēna _____

7. rēmī aptī _____

E. Fill in the blanks with five English words that are derivatives of this week's vocabulary. Write the derivative, then write its Latin root in parentheses. The first one is done for you.

1. _____undulate (unda)_____   4. _____

2. _____   5. _____

3. _____   6. _____

F. Label each declension and complete the chants.

_____ DECLENSION

	SINGULAR	PLURAL
NOM.	-a	
GEN.		
DAT.		
ACC.		
ABL.		

_____ DECLENSION

	SINGULAR	PLURAL
NOM.	-us	
GEN.		
DAT.		
ACC.		
ABL.		

2ND DECLENSION _____

	SINGULAR	PLURAL
NOM.	-um	
GEN.		
DAT.		
ACC.		
ABL.		

Choose one noun from each declension from this week's list and decline them below.

FIRST DECLENSION

	SINGULAR	PLURAL
NOM.		
GEN.		
DAT.		
ACC.		
ABL.		

SECOND DECLENSION

	SINGULAR	PLURAL
NOM.		
GEN.		
DAT.		
ACC.		
ABL.		

SECOND DECLENSION NEUTER

	SINGULAR	PLURAL
NOM.		
GEN.		
DAT.		
ACC.		
ABL.		

Now, go back to the nouns you've just declined and underline all of the endings. (Remember, the part of the noun that doesn't change is called the *base*.)

G. Look up these words in a Latin dictionary. For each word, give it's genitive singular ending, gender (M, F, or N), base, and declension (1 or 2).

	NOUN	GENITIVE	GENDER	BASE	DECLENSION
1.	diēcula				
2.	rubus				
3.	ientāculum				
4.	scriptūra				
5.	fīliolus				
6.	columbus				
7.	sūdārium				
8.	Narnia				

H. All the words listed below are in French, but all of them are related to words you've learned this week. Use your Word List to figure out what each word means in English!

1. aile _____

2. astre _____

3. serein _____

4. fleuve _____

5. ancre _____

I. Answer the questions about this week's quotation.

1. What does *Ālīs volat propriīs* mean? _____

2. Which state uses this as their motto? _____

WEEK 10

Word List

NOUNS

1. pulvīnus, -ī (m) . . . . pillow, cushion
2. somnus, -ī (m) . . . . sleep

ADJECTIVES

3. antīquus, -a, -um . . . . . . ancient
4. beātus, -a, -um . . . . happy, blessed
5. famēlicus, -a, -um . . . . . . hungry
6. foedus, -a, -um . . . . horrible, ugly
7. maculōsus, -a, -um . . . . . spotted, stained
8. pulcher, -chra, -chrum . . . beautiful
9. pūrpureus, -a, -um . . . . . . purple
10. pūrus, -a, -um . . . . pure, clean
11. quiētus, -a, -um . . . . quiet, sleeping
12. rīdiculus, -a, -um . . . . . . funny, amusing
13. tardus, -a, -um . . . . slow

VERBS

14. crescō, crescere . . . . I grow, arise
15. somniō, somniāre . . . . . I dream
16. sum . . . . I am

Chant:

Sum, *I am*—Present Active Irregular Verb

LATIN

	SINGULAR	PLURAL
1ST	sum	sumus
2ND	es	estis
3RD	est	sunt

ENGLISH

	SINGULAR	PLURAL
1ST	I am	we are
2ND	you are	you all are
3RD	he/she/it is	they are

 Quotation: *verbatim*—"word for word"

WEEK 10 *Derivatives:*

Quotation:

Weekly Worksheet 10

name: _____

A. Fill in the blanks.

1. An adjective modifies a _____ or _____.

2. An adjective answers the questions _____ kind? _____ one? or how _____?

3. In Latin, _____ follows a linking verb and describes a subject noun.

4. It matches the subject noun in _____, number, and _____.

5. Give an example in Latin of a linking verb: _____

7. In Latin sentences with predicate adjectives, does the verb usually appear at the beginning, in the middle, or at the end of the sentence? _____

B. Translate each English adjective into Latin, in the gender given. Use the *nominative singular* form. The first one is done for you.

1. feminine: *wonderful* ____mīra____
2. masculine: *hungry* _____
3. feminine: *purple* _____
4. masculine: *happy* _____
5. neuter: *horrible* _____
6. neuter: *amusing* _____

C. Give the base for each of these nouns.

1. ancora _____
2. fluvius _____
3. pulvīnus _____
4. prōra _____
5. astrum _____
6. āla _____

D. Underline the adjective that goes with the noun and then translate the phrase.

NOUN	ADJECTIVE	TRANSLATION
1. Pulvīnus	pulcher / pulchrum	_____

2. Somnus   quiētum / quiētus   _____

3. Ancora   antīqua / antīquae   _____

4. Sciūrī   rīdicula / rīdiculī _____

5. Vēla   maculōsa / maculōsae _____

6. Coma   ūmida / ūmidum   _____

E. Answer the following questions about *cresco, crescere*.

1. Which conjugation is *cresco* in? _____

2. Which family is it in? _____

3. What is the stem of *cresco*? _____

4. Does *cresco* conjugate like *amō, videō,* or *ducō*? _____

Conjugate and translate *cresco* in the present tense.

LATIN

	SINGULAR	PLURAL
1ST		
2ND		
3RD		

ENGLISH

	SINGULAR	PLURAL
1ST		
2ND		
3RD		

F. Conjugate and translate *sum* in the present tense, then answer the questions.

LATIN

	SINGULAR	PLURAL
1ST		
2ND		
3RD		

ENGLISH

	SINGULAR	PLURAL
1ST		
2ND		
3RD		

1. Does *sum* conjugate regularly or irregularly? _____

G. Each sentence below uses an adjective and a form of *sum*. Translate each sentence, then write in the parentheses whether the adjective is masculine (M), feminine (F), or neuter (N). The first one is done for you.

1. Est dēliciōsus! _____ It is delicious! _____ (M)

2. Sum famēlica. _____ (   )

3. Es famēlicus. _____ (   )

4. Sunt rīdiculī. _____ (   )

5. Est foedum! _____ (   )

6. Sumus pūrae. _____ (   )

7. Sunt pūrpurea. _____ (   )

H. Translate these sentences. (Hint: It's best to start by finding the verb!)

1. Equus gelidus nat. _____

2. Estis serēnae et aptae. _____

3. Venēnum pūrpureum exanimābit. _____

4. Astrum est serēnum. _____

5. Sciūrus maculōsus somniābat. _____

6. Ōceanī sunt antīquī. _____

7. Harēnae sunt apricae. _____

8. Fēmina pulchra dūcit. _____

9. Cunīculī quiētī olefactānt. _____

10. Coquus est famēlicus. _____

11. Nucleī sunt brūnī. _____

12. Saxum est āridum. _____

13. Parvus ulmus crescit. _____

I. Adjectives decline just like the nouns they modify. Below, decline *tardus* in the masculine and *beātus* in the feminine.

	SINGULAR	PLURAL
NOM.	tardus	
GEN.		
DAT.		
ACC.		
ABL.		

	SINGULAR	PLURAL
NOM.	beata	
GEN.		
DAT.		
ACC.		
ABL.		

Now, decline the phrase below.

	SINGULAR	PLURAL
NOM.		quiētae noctuae
GEN.		
DAT.		
ACC.		
ABL.		

J. Give the stems for the following verbs.

1. somniō, somniāre _____

2. augeō, augēre _____

3. hiemō, hiemāre _____

4. dūcō, dūcere _____

5. valeō, valēre _____

6. instō, instāre _____

WEEK 11

Word List

NOUNS

1. Deus, -ī (m) . . . . God
2. familia, -ae (f) . . . . . . family, household
3. germāna, -ae (f) . . . . . sister
4. germānus, -ī (m) . . . . . brother
5. liber, librī (m) . . . . book
6. verbum, -ī (n) . . . . word
7. vir, virī (m) . . . . man

ADJECTIVES

8. aeternus, -a, -um . . . . . eternal
9. bonus, -a, -um . . . . . . good
10. caecus, -a, -um . . . . . blind
11. iūstus, -a, -um . . . . . . just, righteous
12. laetus, -a, -um . . . . . . happy, joyful

VERBS

13. cōgitō, cōgitāre . . . . . I think
14. dēclārō, dēclārāre . . . I declare, explain
15. flō, flāre . . . . I blow, breathe
16. gaudeō, gaudēre . . . . I rejoice
17. iūdicō, iūdicāre . . . . . I judge
18. lūgeō, lūgēre . . . . . . I grieve, mourn
19. mūtō, mūtāre . . . . . . I change
20. spērō, spērāre . . . . . . I hope

Chant:

Dūcam, *I will lead*—Future Active Third Conjugation or "e" Family Verb

LATIN

	SINGULAR	PLURAL
1ST	dūcam	dūcēmus
2ND	dūcēs	dūcētis
3RD	dūcet	dūcent

ENGLISH

	SINGULAR	PLURAL
1ST	I will lead	we will lead
2ND	you will lead	you all will lead
3RD	he/she/it will lead	they will lead

(Continued on next page)

Latin Primer Book 2

Quotation:

ipsissima verba—"the very words"

WEEK 11 *Derivatives:* _____

_____
_____
_____
_____
_____
_____
_____
_____
_____
_____
_____
_____
_____
_____

Quotation: _____
_____
_____

Weekly Worksheet 11

name: _____

A. Conjugate and translate this week's verb chant, then answer the questions about it.

LATIN

	SINGULAR	PLURAL
1ST	dūcam	
2ND		
3RD		

ENGLISH

	SINGULAR	PLURAL
1ST	I will lead	
2ND		
3RD		

1. Which conjugation is *dūcō, ducere* in? _____

2. Which family is it in? _____

3. How do you find the stem of *dūcō*? _____
_____

4. What is the stem of *dūcō, dūcere*? _____

B. Translate these review words from memory!

1. virga _____

2. peccō _____

3. latebra _____

4. pontus _____

5. poēta _____

6. mālum _____

7. turba _____

8. inimīcus _____

9. fuscina _____

10. cēna _____

11. ambulō _____

12. sella _____

13. epistula _____

14. armentum _____

15. censeō _____

16. ūva _____

17. brūnus _____

18. valeō _____

C. Using this week's Word List, look at the genitive forms of these nouns and give the base for each.

1. familia _____   4. verbum _____

2. germana _____   5. germanus _____

3. liber _____   6. vir _____

D. For each word, give the nominative singular and plural forms, then tell which declension each word is in (1, 2, or 2N). The first one is done for you.

	ENGLISH	LATIN SINGULAR	LATIN PLURAL	DECLENSION
1.	cushion	pulvīnus	pulvīnī	2
2.	sister			
3.	brother			
4.	household			
5.	word			
6.	man			
7.	book			
8.	star			
9.	owl			

E. Give the masculine, feminine, and neuter singular forms of these adjectives in Latin.

	ADJECTIVE	MASCULINE	FEMININE	NEUTER
1.	happy			
2.	blind			
3.	eternal			

F. Decline *bonus liber*.

	SINGULAR	PLURAL
NOM.		
GEN.		
DAT.		
ACC.		
ABL.		

G. Below are seven English derivatives. Draw a line to match each word to its Latin root!

1. cogitation   iūdicō

2. mutant   cogitō

3. virile   Deus

4. verbal   verbum

5. eternal   mūtō

6. judication   vir

7. Deity   aeternus

H. Underline the ending of each verb and translate it.

1. cogitātis _____   2. flō _____

3. gaudent _____   5. declārāmus _____

4. iūdicat _____   6. mūtat _____

I. Translate these sentences into English.

1. Germānus bonus gaudet. _____

Latin Primer Book 2

2. Virī laetī sperant. _____

3. Puella caeca dūcet. _____

4. Germānae salsae dēclārābunt. _____

5. Pulvīnī sunt maculōsī. _____

6. Deus est iūstus et bonus. _____

7. Fluvius gelidus properat. _____

8. Fīliī iūstī exsultant. _____

9. Pontus est serēnus. _____

10. Vir est caecus. _____

J. Conjugate and translate each word in the tense given.

crescō, crescere—Future Active

LATIN

	SINGULAR	PLURAL
1ST		
2ND		
3RD		

ENGLISH

SINGULAR	PLURAL

gaudeō, gaudēre—Present Active

LATIN

	SINGULAR	PLURAL
1ST		
2ND		
3RD		

ENGLISH

SINGULAR	PLURAL

WEEK 12

Word List

NOUNS

1. avia, -ae (f) . . . . grandmother
2. avus, -ī (m) . . . . grandfather
3. littera, -ae (f) . . . . letter of the alphabet,
   PLURAL: litterae, -ārum . . . letter, epistle
4. matrimonium, -ī (n) . . . marriage

ADVERBS

5. certātim . . . . eagerly
6. crās . . . . tomorrow
7. herī . . . . yesterday
8. hodiē . . . . today
9. minūtātim . . . . gradually, bit by bit
10. nōn . . . . not
11. satis . . . . enough
12. semper . . . . always
13. simul . . . . at the same time

VERBS

14. agō, agere . . . . I do, act
15. scrībō, scrībere . . . . . I write
16. serō, serere . . . . I sow, plant
17. vīvō, vīvere . . . . I live

Chant:

Dūcēbam, *I was leading*—Imperfect Active Third Conjugation or "e" Family Verb

LATIN

	SINGULAR	PLURAL
1ST	dūcēbam	dūcēbāmus
2ND	dūcēbās	dūcēbātis
3RD	dūcēbat	dūcēbant

ENGLISH

	SINGULAR	PLURAL
1ST	I was leading	we were leading
2ND	you were leading	you all were leading
3RD	he/she/it was leading	they were leading

(Continued on next page)

> **Quotation:**
> *Iam satis est!*—"That's enough already!"

WEEK 12 *Derivatives:* _____

_____

_____

_____

_____

_____

_____

_____

_____

_____

_____

_____

_____

_____

_____

Quotation: _____

_____

_____

Weekly Worksheet 12

name:

A. Conjugate and translate this week's verb chant, then answer the questions about it.

LATIN

	SINGULAR	PLURAL
1ST		
2ND	dūcēbās	
3RD		

ENGLISH

	SINGULAR	PLURAL
1ST		
2ND		
3RD		

1. What is the tense of this chant? _____

2. Which conjugation is *dūcō, ducere* in? _____

3. Which family is it in? _____

B. Fill in the imperfect tense endings. Then conjugate *flō, flāre* in the imperfect tense and translate it.

	SINGULAR	PLURAL
1ST		
2ND	-bās	
3RD		

LATIN

	SINGULAR	PLURAL
1ST		
2ND		
3RD		

ENGLISH

	SINGULAR	PLURAL
1ST		
2ND		
3RD		

C. Fill in the blanks.

1. An adverb can modify a _____, an _____, or another _____.

2. An adverb answers the questions _____? _____? _____? or to what extent?

D. Translate these sentences.

1. Germāna caeca certātim sperat. _____

2. Deus semper est bonus. _____

3. Germānī crās serent. _____

4. Fābula est mīra. _____

5. Sumus aptī. _____

6. Avus herī scribēbat. _____

7. Astrum nōn est serēnum. _____

8. Avus et avia simul ridēbant. _____

9. Estis laetī. _____

10. Satis agis. _____

E. Fill in the chart's missing labels, then look up the word *puer* in Word List 1. Using the information given there, decline *puer* below.

F. Fill in the blank with the correct form of each word.

1. Nominative singular for *grandfather*: _____

2. Base of the noun that means *anchor*: _____

3. Base of the noun that means *book*: _____

4. First principle part of the verb that means *I live*: _____

5. The verb form that means *he lives*: _____

6. Masculine form of the adjective meaning *eternal*: _____

7. Feminine form of the adjective meaning *blind*: _____

8. Neuter form of the adjective that means *calm*: _____

9. Base of the adjective that means *suitable*: _____

G. Translate each verb, and give its stem and conjugation (1, 2, or 3). The first one is done for you.

	VERB	TRANSLATION	STEM	CONJUGATION
1.	peccāmus	we sin	peccā-	1
2.	gaudet			
3.	crescitis			
4.	lūgēs			
5.	somniābō			
6.	scrībēbātis			
7.	agō			
8.	flābant			

Latin Primer Book 2

H. Give the base for each of these nouns.

1. liber _____
2. matrimonium _____
3. vir _____
4. avia _____
5. pulvīnus _____
6. astrum _____

I. Conjugate the following words in the present, future, and imperfect tenses.

Present Active

FIRST CONJUGATION

	SINGULAR	PLURAL
1ST	mūtō	
2ND		
3RD		

SECOND CONJUGATION

	SINGULAR	PLURAL
1ST	lūgeō	
2ND		
3RD		

THIRD CONJUGATION

	SINGULAR	PLURAL
1ST	vīvō	
2ND		
3RD		

Future Active

FIRST CONJUGATION

	SINGULAR	PLURAL
1ST		
2ND		
3RD		

SECOND CONJUGATION

	SINGULAR	PLURAL
1ST		
2ND		
3RD		

THIRD CONJUGATION

	SINGULAR	PLURAL
1ST		
2ND		
3RD		

Imperfect Active

FIRST CONJUGATION

	SINGULAR	PLURAL
1ST		
2ND		
3RD		

SECOND CONJUGATION

	SINGULAR	PLURAL
1ST		
2ND		
3RD		

THIRD CONJUGATION

	SINGULAR	PLURAL
1ST		
2ND		
3RD		

WEEK 13

Word List

NOUNS

1. balatrō, balatrōnis (m) . . jester, clown
2. caper, caprī (m) . . . . . . billy goat
3. cauda, -ae (f) . . . . tail
4. cavea, -ae (f) . . . . cage, animal den
5. circus, -ī (m) . . . . circle, racecourse
6. ariēs, arietis (m) . . . . . ram
7. elephantus, -ī (m) . . . . elephant
8. flagellum, -ī (n) . . . . . whip
9. mannus, -ī (m) . . . . . . pony
10. pābulum, -ī (n) . . . . . fodder, food for animals
11. tigris, tigridis (m/f) . . . tiger
12. trochus, -ī (m) . . . . . . hoop for games

VERBS

13. currō, currere . . . . . . I run
14. pāreō, pārēre . . . . . . I obey
15. rudō, rudere . . . . I roar, bellow, bray

Chant:
Third Declension Noun Endings

	LATIN			ENGLISH	
	SINGULAR	PLURAL		SINGULAR	PLURAL
NOM.	x	-ēs		a, the *noun*	the *nouns*
GEN.	-is	-um		of the *noun*, the *noun's*	of the *nouns*, the *nouns'*
DAT.	-ī	-ibus		to, for the *noun*	to, for the *nouns*
ACC.	-em	-ēs		the *noun*	the *nouns*
ABL.	-e	-ibus		by, with, from the *noun*	by, with, from the *nouns*

 Quotation:
Circus Maximus—"Greatest Circus"

WEEK 13 *Derivatives:*

Quotation:

Weekly Worksheet 13

name: _____

A. Complete the chant for this week and answer the questions about it.

	SINGULAR	PLURAL

1. Which ending tells you a noun's declension? _____

2. The genitive ending for the third declension is _____.

3. The genitive ending for the second declension is _____.

4. The genitive ending for the first declension is _____.

B. Decline *ariēs* and *tigris* in the chart below, then answer the questions.

	SINGULAR	PLURAL
NOM.	ariēs	
GEN.		
DAT.		
ACC.		
ABL.		

	SINGULAR	PLURAL
NOM.	tigris	
GEN.		
DAT.		
ACC.		
ABL.		

1. Which declension are *ariēs* and *tigris* in? _____

2. How can you tell? _____

C. Translate these sentences into English.

1. Elephantus albus certātim ambulābit. _____

2. Est magnus. _____

3. Mannus brunus appāret. _____

4. Statim pāret et currit. _____

5. Puerī et puellae exsultant. _____

6. Simul rīdēmus. _____

7. Caper maculōsus est famēlicus. _____

8. Tigrēs spectant et rudunt. _____

9. Balatrōnēs salsī semper clāmant. _____

10. Semper sunt rīdiculī. _____

D. Give the masculine, feminine, and neuter nominative singular of these adjectives in Latin.

	ADJECTIVE	MASCULINE	FEMININE	NEUTER
1.	quiet			
2.	joyful			
3.	horrible			
4.	sunny			
5.	cold			

E. For each noun, write in the blank whether it is in the first declension (1), second declension (2), second declension neuter (2N), or third declension (3).

1. pābulum, -ī _____ 3. ariēs, arietis _____

2. circus, -ī _____ 4. cauda, -ae _____

5. tigris, tigridis _____ 8. balatrō, balatrōnis _____

6. caper, caprī _____ 9. matrimonium, -ī _____

7. cavea, -ae _____ 10. liber, librī _____

F. Label the picture using the words below. All of the words should be used once. (Hint: Some of them are review words from last year.)

| puer | leō | ursa | elephantus | circus |
| trochus | equus | tigris | puella | |

G. Conjugate and translate *currō* in the present, future, and imperfect tenses.

Present Active

LATIN

	SINGULAR	PLURAL
1ST	currō	
2ND		
3RD		

ENGLISH

	SINGULAR	PLURAL
1ST	I run	
2ND		
3RD		

Future Active

LATIN

	SINGULAR	PLURAL
1ST		
2ND		
3RD		

ENGLISH

	SINGULAR	PLURAL
1ST		
2ND		
3RD		

Imperfect Active

LATIN

	SINGULAR	PLURAL
1ST		
2ND		
3RD		

ENGLISH

	SINGULAR	PLURAL
1ST		
2ND		
3RD		

H. Answer the questions about this week's quotation.

1. What Latin phrase means "the greatest circus"? _____

2. Which word means "greatest"? _____

3. Was the Roman circus like our circuses today? _____

WEEK 14

Word List

NOUNS

1. insidiae, -ārum (f) . . . . . . ambush, trap, plot
2. rēgīna, -ae (f) . . . . queen
3. rēx, rēgis (m) . . . . king
4. servus, -ī (m) . . . . slave, servant

ADJECTIVES

5. honestus, -a, -um . . . . . . honorable
6. improbus, -a, -um . . . . . . wicked

VERBS

7. accūsō, accūsāre . . . . . . I accuse, blame
8. administrō, administrāre . . I help, manage
9. arō, arāre . . . . I plow
10. dubitō, dubitāre . . . . I doubt, hesitate
11. explōrō, explōrāre . . . I find out, explore
12. intrō, intrāre . . . . I enter
13. līberō, līberāre . . . . . . I set free
14. narrō, narrāre . . . . . I tell, relate, recount
15. nuntiō, nuntiāre . . . . . I announce, declare
16. obsecrō, obsecrāre . . . I beg, implore
17. recuperō, recuperāre . . I recover
18. regnō, regnāre . . . . . I rule, govern, reign
19. rogō, rogāre . . . . I ask
20. vocō, vocāre . . . . . . I call, summon, invite

Chant:

No new chant this week.

Quotation:

Vīvat rēx!—"Long live the king!"

WEEK 14 *Derivatives:*

Quotation:

Weekly Worksheet 14

name: _____

A. Conjugate the following words in the present, future, and imperfect tenses.

Present Active

FIRST CONJUGATION

	SINGULAR	PLURAL
1ST	arō	
2ND		
3RD		

SECOND CONJUGATION

	SINGULAR	PLURAL
1ST	audeō	
2ND		
3RD		

THIRD CONJUGATION

	SINGULAR	PLURAL
1ST	rudō	
2ND		
3RD		

Future Active

FIRST CONJUGATION

	SINGULAR	PLURAL
1ST		
2ND		
3RD		

SECOND CONJUGATION

	SINGULAR	PLURAL
1ST		
2ND		
3RD		

THIRD CONJUGATION

	SINGULAR	PLURAL
1ST		
2ND		
3RD		

Imperfect Active

FIRST CONJUGATION

	SINGULAR	PLURAL
1ST		
2ND		
3RD		

SECOND CONJUGATION

	SINGULAR	PLURAL
1ST		
2ND		
3RD		

THIRD CONJUGATION

	SINGULAR	PLURAL
1ST		
2ND		
3RD		

B. Circle the subject noun, underline the verb, and draw a box around adjectives; leave adverbs unmarked. Then translate these sentences.

1. Servus minūtātim recuperābit. _____

2. Rex certātim intrābit. _____

3. Amicī aliēnī dubitant. _____

4. Balatrō rīdiculus nuntiābit. _____

5. Avus improbus accūsābat. _____

6. Tigris nōn est contentus. _____

7. Rēx nōn arat. _____

8. Nuntius aptus ambulābit. _____

9. Rēx iūstus non peccābit. _____

10. Lupus salsus rogāt. _____

C. Circle the correct meaning of these English words by considering their Latin sources, all of which are words on your current list.

1. *Arable* land is land that _____.

   a) can be cultivated   b) belongs to many people   c) can be inherited

2. A *narrator* in a play _____.

   a) is the lead actor   b) is a starving stagehand   c) tells of events instead of acting them out

3. If Sally is *recuperating,* she is _____.

   a) planning   b) pouring more tea   c) getting well after being sick

4. If something is *indubitable*, it is _____.

   a) so clear it cannot be doubted   b) impossible to believe   c) wicked

5. If someone is being *interrogated,* it means they're being _____.

   a) followed   b) questioned   c) set free

D. For each noun, write in the blank whether it is in the first declension (1), second declension (2), second declension neuter (2N), or third declension (3).

1. insidiae, -ārum _____
2. trochus, -ī _____
3. rēgīna, -ae _____
4. pābulum, -ī _____
5. ariēs, arietis _____

6. servus, -ī _____
7. rēx, rēgis _____
8. flagellum, -ī _____
9. littera, -ae _____
10. avus, -ī _____

E. Answer the following questions.

ITALIAN	SPANISH	FRENCH
re e regina	rey y reina	roi et reine

1. The phrases above say the same thing in different Romance languages. Use your knowledge of Latin to guess what they mean! _____

2. How would you write this phrase in Latin? _____

F. *Pēs* and *mater* are words you learned last year. Find their genitive forms in a Latin dictionary and decline them below. Include their gender and declension.

DECLENSION _____ GENDER _____

	SINGULAR	PLURAL
NOM.	pēs	
GEN.		
DAT.		
ACC.		
ABL.		

DECLENSION _____ GENDER _____

	SINGULAR	PLURAL
NOM.	mater	
GEN.		
DAT.		
ACC.		
ABL.		

G. Translate these phrases and sentences from English into Latin.

1. the wicked trap _____

2. horse and pony _____

3. The king will reign. _____

4. The queen is not recovering. _____

5. An honorable slave is plowing. _____

6. The dog is exploring eagerly. _____

H. Give the stem of each verb and which conjugation it's in. The first one is done for you.

	VERB	STEM	CONJUGATION
1.	accūsō, accūsāre	accūsā-	1
2.	obsecrō, obsecrāre		
3.	rudō, rudere		
4.	pāreō, pārēre		
5.	nuntiō, nuntiāre		
6.	intrō, intrāre		
7.	currō, currere		
8.	gaudeō, gaudēre		

I. Answer the following questions about this week's quotation.

1. How do you say "Long live the king!" in Latin? _____

2. Which word means "king"? _____

WEEK 15

Word List

NOUNS

1. aranea, -ae (f) . . . . .spider
2. bestiola, -ae (f) . . . . .insect
3. caput, capitis (n) . . . . . . .head
4. cornix, cornicis (f) . . . . . .crow
5. corpus, corporis (n) . . . . .body
6. crūs, crūris (n) . . . . .leg
7. musca, -ae (f) . . . . .fly
8. pinna, -ae (f) . . . . .feather, wing
9. vulnus, vulneris (n). . . . . .wound

ADJECTIVES

10. caeruleus, -a, -um . . . . .blue
11. flavus, -a, -um . . . . .yellow, blond

VERBS

12. fīgō, fīgere . . . . .I fasten, attach, make firm
13. mittō, mittere . . . . .I send, let go
14. reptō, reptāre . . . . .I crawl, creep
15. scalpō, scalpere . . . . . . .I carve, scratch

Chant:

Third Declension Neuter Noun Endings

	LATIN		ENGLISH	
	SINGULAR	PLURAL	SINGULAR	PLURAL
NOM.	x	-a	a, the *noun*	the *nouns*
GEN.	-is	-um	of the *noun*, the *noun's*	of the *nouns*, the *nouns'*
DAT.	-ī	-ibus	to, for the *noun*	to, for the *nouns*
ACC.	x	-a	the *noun*	the *nouns*
ABL.	-e	-ibus	by, with, from the *noun*	by, with, from the *nouns*

(Continued on next page)

Latin Primer Book 2

> **Quotation:**
> *Cornicum oculōs configere*—"To peck the eyes of crows"
> (i.e., to give someone a taste of their own medicine)

WEEK 15 *Derivatives:* _____

_____

Quotation: _____

Weekly Worksheet 15

name: _____

A. Complete the chant for this week and answer the questions about it.

	SINGULAR	PLURAL

1. Which ending tells you a noun's declension? _____

2. The genitive ending for the third declension is _____.

3. The genitive ending for the third declension neuter is _____.

4. The genitive ending for the second declension is _____.

5. The genitive ending for the first declension is _____.

B. Decline *crūs* and *vulnus* in the chart below, then answer the questions.

	SINGULAR	PLURAL
NOM.	crūs	
GEN.		
DAT.		
ACC.		
ABL.		

	SINGULAR	PLURAL
NOM.	vulnus	
GEN.		
DAT.		
ACC.		
ABL.		

Latin Primer Book 2

1. Which declension are *crūs* and *vulnus* in? _____

2. How can you tell? _____

3. What gender are *crūs* and *vulnus*? _____

C. Decline *cornix* and *rēx* below.

	SINGULAR	PLURAL
NOM.	cornix	
GEN.		
DAT.		
ACC.		
ABL.		

	SINGULAR	PLURAL
NOM.	rēx	
GEN.		
DAT.		
ACC.		
ABL.		

D. Label the picture using the Latin words below.

pinna   cornix   crūs   caput   corpus

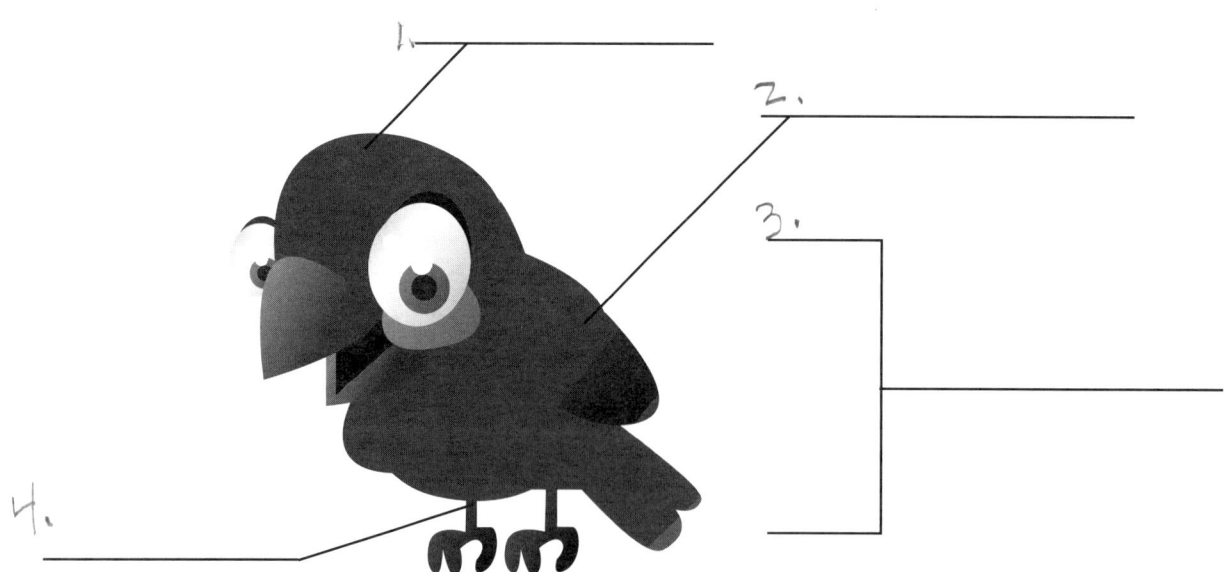

This animal is called a _____.

E. Underline the adjective that matches the noun's number and gender, then translate the phrase.

NOUN	ADJECTIVE	TRANSLATION
1. Pinna	flava / flavae	
2. Vulnera	caeruleae / caerulea	
3. Caput	flavus / flavum	
4. Crūs	magna / magnum	
5. Bestiola	parva / parvum	
6. Cornicēs	improbī / improbae	
7. Insidiae	mīra / mīrae	
8. Rēx	honestus / honestum	
9. Servus	famēlicus / famēlica	
10. Tigridēs	famēlicī / famēlica	

F. Translate the following sentences into English.

1. Araneae caeruleae reptant. _____

2. Balatrō rīdiculus explōrābat. _____

3. Minūtātim scalpō. _____

4. Circus est magnus et lātus. _____

5. Rēgīna flava certātim intrat. _____

6. Semper administrās. _____

7. Simul serēbāmus. _____

8. Hortus minūtātim crescent. _____

9. Caper magnus oppugnat. _____

10. Elephantus parvus et cornicēs volant. _____

G. Translate the following phrases and sentences into English.

1. the spotted insects _____

2. a little wound _____

3. The blue fly is not crawling. _____

4. A blind crow was scratching. _____

5. The king and queen will govern. _____

H. Match the English derivative with its Latin root.

1. captain   mittō

2. pinnacle   reptō

3. liberate   caput

4. reptile   rogō

5. interrogate   līberō

6. missile   pinna

I. Give the stem of each verb, its conjugation, and its family.

	VERB	STEM	CONJUGATION	FAMILY
1.	reptō, reptāre			
2.	pāreō, pārēre			
3.	confīgō, confīgere			
4.	gaudeō, gaudēre			
5.	rudō, rudere			

WEEK 16

Word List

NOUNS

1. argūmentum, -ī (n) . . . . . proof, evidence
2. discipulus, -ī (m) . . . . . . apprentice, student
3. iūs, iūris (n) . . . . justice, right, law
4. lacrima, -ae (f) . . . . tear
5. magister, magistrī (m) . . teacher (male)
6. magistra, -ae (f) . . . . . . teacher (female)
7. pax, pācis (f) . . . . peace

ADJECTIVES

8. contentus, -a, -um . . . . . satisfied, content
9. firmus, -a, -um . . . . . . strong, firm, steadfast

VERBS

10. erō . . . . I will be
11. fleō, flēre . . . . I weep
12. moneō, monēre . . . . . I warn
13. repudiō, repudiāre . . . . I reject, scorn
14. respondeō, respondēre . I respond, answer
15. sedeō, sedēre . . . . I sit
16. timeō, timēre . . . . I fear
17. videō, vidēre . . . . I see

Chant:

Erō, *I will be*—Future Active of *Sum*
Irregular Verb

LATIN			ENGLISH	
	SINGULAR	PLURAL	SINGULAR	PLURAL
1ST	erō	erimus	I will be	we will be
2ND	eris	eritis	you will be	you all will be
3RD	erit	erunt	he/she/it will be	they will be

Quotation:

No new quotation this week.

WEEK 16 *Derivatives:*

Weekly Worksheet 16

name: _____

A. Conjugate *sum* in the present active.

LATIN

	SINGULAR	PLURAL
1ST	sum	
2ND		
3RD		

ENGLISH

	SINGULAR	PLURAL
1ST		
2ND		
3RD		

1. Is *sum* a regular or irregular verb? _____

2. Is *sum* a verb ending or a complete verb? _____

B. Conjugate and translate *sum* in the future active. Try to do it from memory!

LATIN

	SINGULAR	PLURAL
1ST		
2ND		
3RD		

ENGLISH

	SINGULAR	PLURAL
1ST		
2ND		
3RD		

3. Is *erō* a regular or irregular verb? _____

4. Is *erō* an action verb or a being verb? _____

C. Fill in the blanks.

1. A _____ adjective follows a _____ verb and describes a subject noun.

2. A predicate _____ follows a linking verb and identifies or _____ the subject noun.

3. Which Latin case do you use for this part of speech? _____

4. Which Latin case do you use for the subject? _____

D. These are nouns you learned last year. They are grouped by whether they name a person, place, or thing. Give the English translation for each word. (If you need to use your Latin dictionary, do!)

PERSON

1. praefectus _____

2. Iesus _____

3. lēgātus _____

4. captīvus _____

5. cīvis _____

PLACE

6. vīcus _____

7. forum _____

8. patria _____

9. campus _____

10. ecclēsia _____

THING

11. sagitta _____

12. patientia _____

13. praemium _____

14. donum _____

15. fossa _____

E. In each English sentence, underline the subject and circle the predicate noun. Then translate the predicate noun into Latin and write it in the blank. (Hint: Remember which case the predicate noun takes!)

1. Fred is my older brother. _____

2. Shakespeare is a famous poet. _____

3. One day the little nut will be an elm tree. _____

4. Tarantulas are huge, hairy spiders! _____

5. This is my favorite pillow in the world. _____

F. Translate these short sentences. Be careful about the person and tense of the "being" verb.

1. Sum magistra. _____

2. Estis discipulī. _____

3. Erunt laetī. _____

4. Erimus balatrōnēs! _____

5. Nōn erō rēx. _____

6. Erit firmus. _____

G. Underline the adjective that matches the noun's number and gender, then translate the phrase.

NOUN	ADJECTIVE	TRANSLATION
1. Magister	firmus / firmī	
2. Pax	pulcher / pulchra	
3. Vulnus	caeruleus / caeruleum	
4. Lacrimae	laeta / laetae	
5. Corpus	aptus / aptum	

H. Label each noun's declension (1, 2, or 3) and gender (M, F, or N). Then decline it.

DECLENSION _____ GENDER _____

	SINGULAR	PLURAL
NOM.	magister	
GEN.		
DAT.		
ACC.		
ABL.		

DECLENSION _____ GENDER _____

	SINGULAR	PLURAL
NOM.	iūs	
GEN.		
DAT.		
ACC.		
ABL.		

DECLENSION _____ GENDER _____

	SINGULAR	PLURAL
NOM.	pax	
GEN.		
DAT.		
ACC.		
ABL.		

DECLENSION _____ GENDER _____

	SINGULAR	PLURAL
NOM.	argūmentum	
GEN.		
DAT.		
ACC.		
ABL.		

Latin Primer Book 2

I. Translate these sentences. Circle any *predicate nouns*. You'll notice a couple more words from last year!

1. Rēx bonus respondēbit. _____

2. Germānus est discipulus. _____

3. Iūs nōn est perfectus. _____

4. Fābula erit liber. _____

5. Puerī erunt agricolae. _____

6. Biblia Sacra est liber bonus. _____

7. Iesus est magister et rēx et Dominus. _____

8. Argūmentum est firmum. _____

9. Aranea bona scrībet. _____

10. Cunīculus albus currēbat et properābat. _____

11. Lacrimae erunt ūmidae. _____

12. Germānae nōn sunt aviae. _____

13. Fīlius erit vir. _____

J. Answer the questions, then conjugate and translate *mittō, mittere* in the future active tense.

1. Which conjugation is *mittō* in? _____

2. Which family is *mittō* in? _____

LATIN

	SINGULAR	PLURAL
1ST		
2ND		
3RD		

ENGLISH

	SINGULAR	PLURAL
1ST		
2ND		
3RD		

Unit Three

Unit 3: Goals

By the end of Week 24, you should be able to . . .

- Recognize and translate sentences using first, second, and third declension nouns in the accusative case
- Translate and compose Latin questions
- Translate and compose Latin commands
- Recognize and decline masculine and feminine fourth declension nouns

WEEK 17

Word List

NOUNS

1. captīvus, -ī (m) . . . . . . captive
2. disciplīna, -ae (f) . . . . . instruction, training
3. ferus, -ī (m) . . . . wild animal
4. flūmen, flūminis (n) . . . river
5. habēna, -ae (f) . . . . . . strap, rein
6. īnsula, -ae (f) . . . . island
7. lēgātus, -ī (m) . . . . lieutenant
8. memoria, -ae (f) . . . . . memory
9. patria, -ae (f) . . . . native land
10. stimulus, -ī (m) . . . . . goad, spur
11. villa, -ae (f) . . . . farmhouse, country house

VERBS

12. commemorō, commemorāre . . I remember, mention, call to mind
13. laxō, laxāre . . . . I loosen
14. ornō, ornāre . . . . I equip, decorate
15. retineō, retinēre . . . . . I hold back, retain
16. servō, servāre . . . . . . I save

Chant:

No new chant this week.

Quotation:

No new quotation this week.

WEEK 17 *Derivatives:*

Weekly Worksheet 17

name:

A. Write the full names of the cases in order on these lines. Feel free to look below for a hint!

1. _____

2. _____

3. _____

4. _____

5. _____

B. Label each noun's declension (1, 2, or 3) and gender (M, F, or N). Then decline it.

DECLENSION _____ GENDER _____

	SINGULAR	PLURAL
NOM.	memoria	
GEN.		
DAT.		
ACC.		
ABL.		

DECLENSION _____ GENDER _____

	SINGULAR	PLURAL
NOM.	stimulus	
GEN.		
DAT.		
ACC.		
ABL.		

DECLENSION _____ GENDER _____

	SINGULAR	PLURAL
NOM.	pax	
GEN.		
DAT.		
ACC.		
ABL.		

DECLENSION _____ GENDER _____

	SINGULAR	PLURAL
NOM.	flūmen	
GEN.		
DAT.		
ACC.		
ABL.		

Latin Primer Book 2

Now, go back through the nouns you've just declined and circle the accusative case endings for each one.

C. For each noun, list its declension, gender, and its singular and plural accusative forms. The first one is done for you.

	NOUN	DECLENSION	GENDER	SINGULAR ACCUSATIVE	PLURAL ACCUSATIVE
1.	villa	1	F	villam	villās
2.	īnsula				
3.	lēgātus				
4.	pax				
5.	ferus				
6.	argūmentum				
7.	corpus				
8.	cauda				
9.	elephantus				
10.	tigris				
11.	flagellum				

D. Fill in the blanks.

1. The part of speech that *receives the action of the verb* is called the _____ .

2. Which Latin case do you use for this part of speech? _____

3. Which Latin case do you use for the subject? _____

4. What is the other meaning of *ferus* you learned last year? _____

5. *Ferus* can be used as either a _____ or an _____ .

6. An adjective must always match the _____, number, and _____ of the noun it modifies.

E. For each noun, label whether it is nominative (N) or accusative (A), and whether it's singular (S) or plural (P). The first one is done for you.

1. disciplīnās _____AP_____
2. Deus _____
3. inimīcum _____
4. rēgīnās _____
5. nauta _____
6. villa _____
7. pācem _____
8. insidiae _____
9. magistrōs _____
10. aquam _____
11. lēgātum _____
12. tigridem _____

F. In each English sentence, underline the verb and circle the direct object. Translate the direct object into Latin and write it the blank. (Hint: Remember which case the direct object takes!) The first one is done for you.

1. Once, a lost girl <u>found</u> a (country house) in the woods. _____villam_____

2. Slowly, she opened the door. _____

3. Inside, she saw seven pillows on seven beds. _____

4. And she discovered seven chairs at the table. _____

5. "I will make dinner for these people!" _____

6. But a cruel queen had invented a deadly plot. _____

7. In disguise, the queen offered an apple to the girl. _____

8. She had hidden poison in it. _____

9. The poison killed the girl. _____

10. But you know this story. _____

11. And you remember the happy marriage at the end! _____

G. Translate these Latin sentences.

1. Agricola retinet. _____

2. Captīvī servant. _____

3. Fēminae omant. _____

4. Lēgātus laxat. _____

5. Populus commemorat. _____

6. Lēgātus significat. _____

7. Repudiāmus. _____

H. These sentences include direct objects, which will be in the accusative case. Underline subject nouns and circle direct objects, then translate the sentences into English.

1. Agricola equum retinet. _____

2. Captīvī patriam servant. _____

3. Fēminae villam omant. _____

4. Lēgātus habēnās laxat. _____

5. Populus memoriam commemorat. _____

6. Lēgātus captīvōs significat. _____

7. Pācem repudiāmus. _____

8. Lēgātum nōn timeō. _____

9. Discipulus lacrimās flēbat. _____

10. Aranea muscam nōn līberābit. _____

I. Translate these English sentences into Latin.

1. I remember the island. _____

2. We see the owls. _____

3. The wall holds back the wild animal. _____

4. The elephants obey the clown. _____

WEEK 18

Word List

NOUNS

1. adulēscēns, adulēscentis (m) . young man
2. bōs, bovis (m/f). . . . . ox, bull, cow
3. labor, labōris (m) . . . . work, labor
4. latus, lateris (n). . . . . flank, side
5. ōs, ōris (n) . . . . mouth
6. pēs, pedis (m). . . . . foot
7. pulvis, pulveris (m) . . . . dirt, dust, powder
8. sēmen, sēminis (n). . . . . . . seed

ADJECTIVES

9. pulvereus, -a, -um . . . . dusty, full of dust
10. fessus, -a, -um . . . . . . tired, weary

ADVERBS

11. ūnā. . . . . together, in one

VERBS

12. dō, dāre. . . . . I give
13. edō, edere . . . . I eat
14. iungō, iungere . . . . . I join, unite, yoke
15. quiescō, quiescere . . . I rest, sleep

Chant:
No new chant this week.

> **Quotation:**
> *pulvis in pulverem*—"dust to dust"

WEEK 18 *Derivatives:*

Quotation:

Weekly Worksheet 18

name:

A. Translate these review words into English.

1. verbum _____

2. caelum _____

3. saxum _____

4. vēlum _____

5. folium _____

6. aedificium _____

7. venēnum _____

8. praemium _____

9. bellum _____

10. dōnum _____

B. Label each noun's declension (1, 2, or 3) and gender (M, F, or N). Then decline it.

DECLENSION _____ GENDER _____

	SINGULAR	PLURAL
NOM.	folium	
GEN.		
DAT.		
ACC.		
ABL.		

DECLENSION _____ GENDER _____

	SINGULAR	PLURAL
NOM.	latus	
GEN.		
DAT.		
ACC.		
ABL.		

Now, go back and underline the nominative and accusative forms of each noun. Then answer the following questions.

1. Why do you have to be especially careful when translating neuter nouns? _____

_____

2. When you translate a sentence, which part of speech should you locate first? _____

C. For each noun, list its declension, gender, and its singular and plural accusative forms.

	NOUN	DECLENSION	GENDER	SINGULAR ACCUSATIVE	PLURAL ACCUSATIVE
1.	vulnus				
2.	lacrima				
3.	ōs				
4.	ferus				
5.	pulvis				
6.	iūs				
7.	sēmen				
8.	verbum				

D. Fill in the blanks.

1. The subject of a sentence takes the _____ case.

2. The direct object of a sentence takes the _____ case.

3. The direct object receives the action of the _____.

E. Translate these sentences. Start by underlining the verb, circling the subject, and drawing a box around the direct object.

1. Deus populum commemorābit. _____

2. Populus Deum commemorābit. _____

3. Bovēs agrum arant. _____

4. Adulēscēns frāga et ariēnās edēbat. _____

5. Mūrus magnus aquam retinēbit. _____

6. Lēgātus inimīcum servābit. _____

7. Rēgīna improba pācem repudiat. _____

8. Bovēs ūnā iungēmus. _____

F. Conjugate the following words in the present, future, and imperfect tenses.

Present Active

FIRST CONJUGATION

	SINGULAR	PLURAL
1ST	ornō	
2ND		
3RD		

SECOND CONJUGATION

SINGULAR	PLURAL
fleō	

THIRD CONJUGATION

SINGULAR	PLURAL
edō	

Future Active

FIRST CONJUGATION

	SINGULAR	PLURAL
1ST		
2ND		
3RD		

SECOND CONJUGATION

SINGULAR	PLURAL

THIRD CONJUGATION

SINGULAR	PLURAL

Imperfect Active

FIRST CONJUGATION

	SINGULAR	PLURAL
1ST		
2ND		
3RD		

SECOND CONJUGATION

SINGULAR	PLURAL

THIRD CONJUGATION

SINGULAR	PLURAL

G. Translate these sentences into English. (Hint: Some adjectives will be in the accusative!)

1. Pedēs saepe sunt pulvereī. _____

2. Insidiam improbam crās nuntiābitis. _____

3. Bellum puellās terret. _____

4. Familiae aedificium ornant. _____

5. Lupī famēlicī cervum fessum instant. _____

6. Sciūrī nucluēōs ūnā edunt. _____

7. Saxum fīlius laxat. _____

8. Coquī fungōs odōrātōs olefactant. _____

9. Elephantī flagella semper pārēbunt. _____

10. Agricola bonus sēmena serit. _____

H. Label whether each noun is masculine (M), feminine (F), or neuter (N). Try to do it from memory!

1. balatrō _____   5. pax _____   9. rēx _____

2. servus _____   6. caput _____   10. cornix _____

3. argūmentum _____   7. vulnus _____   11. labor _____

4. flūmen _____   8. crūs _____   12. latus _____

I. Give the masculine, feminine, and neuter *nominative plural* of these adjectives in Latin.

	ADJECTIVE	MASCULINE	FEMININE	NEUTER
1.	strong			
2.	weary			
3.	blond			

WEEK 19

Word List

NOUNS

1. hasta, -ae (f) . . . . spear, lance
2. luxuria, -ae (f) . . . . luxury, extravagance
3. mūnicipium, -ī (n) . . . . free town
4. oppidum, -ī (n) . . . . . . town
5. prōvincia, -ae (f) . . . . . province
6. querēla, -ae (f) . . . . . . complaint, whining
7. stabulum, -ī (n) . . . . . . stall, stable
8. tectum, -ī (n) . . . . roof, ceiling, dwelling
9. victōria, -ae (f) . . . . . . victory

VERBS

10. dēmonstrō, dēmonstrāre . . . . I show
11. exerceō, exercēre . . . . I train, exercise
12. obsideō, obsidēre . . . I remain near, besiege
13. pacō, pacāre . . . . I pacify, subdue
14. removeō, removēre . . I remove, take away
15. vulnerō, vulnerāre . . . I wound

Chant:

No new chant this week.

> **Quotation:**
> *Victōria, nōn praeda*—"Victory, not loot"

WEEK 19 *Derivatives:*

Quotation:

Weekly Worksheet 19

name: _____

A. Label each declension and complete the chants. Then circle all of the accusative endings.

_____ DECLENSION

	SINGULAR	PLURAL
NOM.	-a	
GEN.		
DAT.		
ACC.		
ABL.		

_____ DECLENSION

	SINGULAR	PLURAL
NOM.	-us	
GEN.		
DAT.		
ACC.		
ABL.		

2ND DECLENSION _____

	SINGULAR	PLURAL
NOM.	-um	
GEN.		
DAT.		
ACC.		
ABL.		

_____ DECLENSION

	SINGULAR	PLURAL
NOM.	x	
GEN.		
DAT.		
ACC.		
ABL.		

3RD DECLENSION _____

	SINGULAR	PLURAL
NOM.	x	
GEN.		
DAT.		
ACC.		
ABL.		

B. For each noun, list its declension, gender, and its singular and plural accusative forms.

	NOUN	DECLENSION	GENDER	SINGULAR ACCUSATIVE	PLURAL ACCUSATIVE
1.	mūnicipium				
2.	pēs				
3.	luxuria				

	NOUN	DECLENSION	GENDER	SINGULAR ACCUSATIVE	PLURAL ACCUSATIVE
4.	labor				
5.	querēla				
6.	oppidum				
7.	magister				
8.	ferus				
9.	lacrima				
10.	pax				

C. The following sentences use derivatives. Complete each sentence. Feel free to look back at this week's Word List or use a dictionary if you need help.

1. A knight wearing weak armor is *vulnerable*, meaning he can be _____.

2. The store owner and I had a *quarrel,* because I had a _____ about my purchase.

3. The king gave a *demonstration* of his new army, _____ how ready they were for battle.

D. For each Latin sentence, circle the subject and underline the direct object. Then translate the sentence into English.

1. Lēgātus oppidum obsidet. _____

2. Mūnicipium victōriam commemorābit. _____

3. Lēgātus equum maculōsum pacat. _____

4. Fīliae pulchrae cēnam removēbunt. _____

5. Victōria prōvinciam servābit. _____

6. Armentum dēmonstrō. _____

7. Portam antīquam removēbit. _____

8. Deum semper laudat. _____

9. Fēmina aquam gelidam lībat. _____

10. Equī stabulum astant. _____

11. Morbus colōnōs exanimābit. _____

12. Nimbus magnus oppidum occultat. _____

13. Servī ūvās removēbunt. _____

14. Turba querēlās clamat. _____

15. Nuntium parāmus. _____

16. Provinciam parvam oppugnābunt. _____

E. Underline the direct object in these English sentences. Translate the direct object into Latin and write it in the blank. (Hint: Remember which case the direct object takes!)

1. They will repair the roof on the next sunny day. _____

2. The exhausted deer reached the riverbank. _____

3. Sarah mails one letter every week. _____

4. Fido feared the bull. _____

5. The king chastised the messengers. _____

6. He caught five spiders. _____

F. Here are English sentences and their Latin translations. Each translation contains one word that is incorrect. Cross out that word and write the correct word in the blank.

1. The reins will hold back the horse. *Habēnae equus retinēbunt.* _____

2. The sailor is standing near the lieutenant. *Lēgātum nauta astābit.* _____

3. The slaves are pointing out the islands. *Servī īnsulam significant.* _____

4. Girls will decorate the buildings. *Puellae tectās ornābunt.* _____

Latin Primer Book 2

5. The ships are besieging the island. *Navēs insulam obsidet.* _____

G. Each of the words below comes from a Latin root! Figure out which of your Latin words is the root, and then give its English meaning.

	ITALIAN	SPANISH	FRENCH	LATIN	ENGLISH
1.	vittoria	victoria	victoire		
2.	isola	isleno	ile		
3.	provincia	provincia	province		
4.	memoria	memoria	mémoire		
5.	villa	villa	villa		

H. Fill in the blanks.

1. The _____ case is used for the subject of a Latin sentence.

2. The _____ case is used for the direct object.

3. To discover which delension a noun is in, you check its _____ case.

I. For each English sentence, circle the subject and underline the direct object. Then translate the sentence into Latin.

1. The wild animal is standing near the farmhouse. _____

_____

2. A sailor is pointing out the land. _____

3. The quiver conceals the arrows. _____

4. The spears will wound the wild animal. _____

5. I will take away the bad dinner. _____

WEEK 20

Word List

NOUNS

1. candēla, -ae (f) . . . . . . candle
2. carmen, carminis (n) . . . song, poem
3. cor, cordis (n) . . . . heart
4. flōs, flōris (m) . . . . flower
5. lux, lūcis (f) . . . . light
6. lyra, -ae (f) . . . . lyre
7. tempus, temporis (n) . . time
8. vesper, vesperis (m) . . . evening, evening star

9. virgō, virginis (f) . . . . . maiden
10. vox, vōcis (f) . . . . voice

VERBS

11. cantō, cantāre . . . . . . I sing, play (music)
12. habeō, habēre . . . . . . I have, hold
13. lūdō, lūdere . . . . I play, tease, trick
14. portō, portāre . . . . . . I carry

Chant:

No new chant this week.

Quotation:

Sursum corda—"Lift up your hearts (to God)"

WEEK 20 *Derivatives:*

Quotation:

Weekly Worksheet 20

name: _____

A. Conjugate and translate *sum* in the present and future active tenses. Then answer the question.

Present Active

LATIN

	SINGULAR	PLURAL
1ST		
2ND		
3RD		

ENGLISH

	SINGULAR	PLURAL
1ST		
2ND		
3RD		

Future Active

LATIN

	SINGULAR	PLURAL
1ST		
2ND		
3RD		

ENGLISH

	SINGULAR	PLURAL
1ST		
2ND		
3RD		

1. Is *sum* a regular or irregular verb? _____

B. Fill in the blank with the English translation of each noun. Underline the Latin nouns that could be used as direct objects. (Hint: Watch your declensions!)

1. stellam _____

2. dominōs _____

3. amīcum _____

4. aquilae _____

5. latera _____

6. ripās _____

7. carmina _____

8. lupus _____

9. latebra _____

10. vōcēs _____

C. Underline the adjective that matches the noun's number, gender, and case. Then translate the phrase.

NOUN	ADJECTIVE	TRANSLATION
1. Candēlae	odōrāta / odōrātae	
2. Vox	fessa / fessam	
3. Bovēs	parvōs / parva	
4. Iūs	firmus / firmum	
5. Flōrēs	flavī / flavās	
6. Lūcem	caeruleam / caeruleās	
7. Carmen	rīdiculam / rīdiculum	
8. Stabula	pulverea / pulvereae	

D. Translate these sentences into English.

1. Hastās pulvereās removet. _____
2. Tempus hodiē nōn habeō. _____
3. Fīlia serēna auroram spectat. _____
4. Equus albus stimulōs pārēbit. _____
5. Ferum parvum servānt. _____
6. Puerī trochōs portant. _____
7. Ancoram parvam ventus laxābit. _____
8. Balatrō virōs quiētōs lūdēbat. _____
9. Poēta lyram crās cantābit. _____
10. Aranea muscam minūtātim edit. _____
11. Virgō laeta litterās scribet. _____

12. Puer astrum serēnum dēmonstrat. _____

E. Give the genitive singular form, gender (M, F, or N), declension, and the English translation for each Latin noun.

	NOUN	GENITIVE	GENDER	DECLENSION	TRANSLATION
1.	cor				
2.	oppidum				
3.	vesper				
4.	latus				
5.	lux				
6.	querēla				
7.	candēla				
8.	cibus				

F. Translate these English sentences into Latin.

1. The king is summoning the slave. _____

2. The teacher sees the tears. _____

3. Students are entering the building. _____

4. The lieutenant fears an ambush. _____

5. He will not hesitate. _____

6. The sailors are decorating the bow of the ship. _____
_____

7. The farmers are plowing the land. _____

8. The woman is imploring the queen. _____

G. Conjugate the following words in the present, future, and imperfect tenses.

Present Active

FIRST CONJUGATION

	SINGULAR	PLURAL
1ST	cantō	
2ND		
3RD		

SECOND CONJUGATION

SINGULAR	PLURAL
habeō	

THIRD CONJUGATION

SINGULAR	PLURAL
lūdō	

Future Active

FIRST CONJUGATION

	SINGULAR	PLURAL
1ST		
2ND		
3RD		

SECOND CONJUGATION

SINGULAR	PLURAL

THIRD CONJUGATION

SINGULAR	PLURAL

Imperfect Active

FIRST CONJUGATION

	SINGULAR	PLURAL
1ST		
2ND		
3RD		

SECOND CONJUGATION

SINGULAR	PLURAL

THIRD CONJUGATION

SINGULAR	PLURAL

H. Answer the following questions about this week's quotation.

1. How do you say "Lift up your hearts" in Latin? _____

2. Which word means "hearts"? _____

3. Which two cases could that word be in? _____

WEEK 21

Word List

NOUNS

1. asinus, -ī (m) . . . . donkey
2. crux, crucis (f) . . . . . . cross
3. dux, ducis (m) . . . . . . leader
4. iter, itineris (n) . . . . . . journey
5. moenia, -ium (n, pl) . . . fortifications, city walls
6. nōmen, nōminis (n) . . . name
7. palma, -ae (f) . . . . . . palm of the hand, palm tree
8. princeps, principis (n) . . chief
9. tībia, -ae (f) . . . . flute, pipe
10. vestīmentum, -ī (n) . . . clothing, garment

VERBS

11. flōreō, flōrēre . . . . . . I flourish
12. imperō, imperāre . . . . I order
13. moveō, movēre . . . . . I move
14. vehō, vehere . . . . I carry, ride, convey
15. vibrō, vibrāre . . . . . . I wave, shake

Chant:

No new chant this week.

Quotation:
iustus ut palma flōrēbit—"the just shall flourish as the palm tree"

WEEK 21 *Derivatives:*

Quotation:

Weekly Worksheet 21

name: _____

A. Answer the following questions about Latin sentences.

1. The subject noun always takes the _____ case.

2. In a Latin sentence, the verb is usually at the _____.

3. To form a question in Latin, _____ is added to the first word in the sentence.

4. The first word in a Latin question is usually the _____.

B. Translate these verbs into English.

1. cantābimus _____

2. līberābit _____

3. lūdēmus _____

4. explōrābunt _____

5. obsecrant _____

6. manēbit _____

7. mūtābit _____

8. vibrābitis _____

9. veham _____

10. accusant _____

11. moneō _____

12. recuperābō _____

13. flōrēs _____

14. augent _____

15. dubitant _____

16. repudiat _____

C. Compare the Latin sentences and their translations below. Underline the verb in each Latin sentence and circle the -ne ending in each question.

1. Discipulus repudiat.   *The student is disputing.*
2. Repudiatne discipulus?   *Is the student disputing?*

3. Ventus mūtābit.   *The wind will change.*
4. Mūtābitne ventus?   *Will the wind change?*

5. Fīlia dubitat.   *The daughter is hesitating.*
6. Fīliane dubitat?   *Is the daughter hesitating?*

7. Fīliae magistrās administrābant.   *The daughters were helping the teachers.*
8. Administrābantne fīliae magistrās?   *Were the daughters helping the teachers?*

D. Underline the subject noun that matches the verb. Then translate the question into English.

VERB	SUBJECT NOUN	TRANSLATION
1. Cantābitne	virgō / virginēs ?	
2. Flōrēbuntne	palmae / palmās ?	
3. Rudetne	asinus / asinum ?	
4. Eduntne	bōs / bovēs ?	
5. Obsidetne	dux / ducis ?	
6. Servābitne	iūs / iūra ?	
7. Lūduntne	caprī / caprōs ?	
8. Imperābitne	principe / princeps ?	

E. For each noun, list its declension, gender, and its singular and plural accusative forms.

	NOUN	DECLENSION	GENDER	SINGULAR ACCUSATIVE	PLURAL ACCUSATIVE
1.	nōmen				
2.	tībia				
3.	crux				
4.	flōs				
5.	vestīmentum				
6.	lēgātus				
7.	iter				
8.	lyra				

F. Give each verb's stem and conjugation. The first one is done for you.

1. vehō _____vehe-___3rd_____ 4. quiescō _____

2. habeō _____ 5. pacō _____

3. vibrō _____ 6. iungō _____

G. Label each tense and complete the verb ending chants.

_____ TENSE

	SINGULAR	PLURAL
1ST	-ō	
2ND		
3RD		

_____ TENSE

	SINGULAR	PLURAL
1ST	-bō	
2ND		
3RD		

_____ TENSE

	SINGULAR	PLURAL
1ST	-bam	
2ND		
3RD		

H. Translate the following sentences into English. In each question, underline the verb's *-ne* ending. Some sentences have direct objects—circle the direct objects!

1. Astatne magistra? _____

2. Administrābitne servus? _____

3. Explōrābuntne puerī? _____

4. Accusatne rēgīna? _____

5. Manēbuntne moenia? _____

6. Spectatne magister? _____

7. Timēbatne sagittam germānus? _____

8. Vehitne asinum princeps? _____

9. Familiane cēnam imperat? _____

10. Occupatne terram agricola? _____

Latin Primer Book 2

I. Answer the questions about this week's quotation.

1. How do you say "the just shall flourish as the palm tree" in Latin? _____

_____

2. Which word means "just"? _____

3. Which word means "shall flourish"? _____

J. This is review from last year! Write these numbers in order on the lines: *trēs, quinque, duo, novem, sex, decem, ūnus, quattuor, septem, octō*. (Hint: Feel free to look the numbers up in your Latin dictionary.)

_____

_____

_____

K. Give the masculine, feminine, and neuter *accusative singular* forms of these adjectives in Latin.

	ADJECTIVE	MASCULINE	FEMININE	NEUTER
1.	weary			
2.	strong			
3.	dusty			

L. For each sentence, first underline the verb, then circle the subject. (Hint: The verb may be split up. Watch for "will" and "were"!) Then translate it into Latin.

1. Will the anchor move? _____

2. Is the effort helping? _____

3. Is the river cold? _____

4. Were you asking? _____

5. Will the flowers flourish? _____

WEEK 22

Word List

NOUNS

1. architectus, -ī (m) . . . . . architect, inventor
2. centaurus, -ī (m) . . . . . centaur
3. cyclops, cyclōpis (m) . . cyclops
4. dracō, dracōnis (m) . . . dragon
5. fīlum, -ī (n) . . . . thread, string
6. gigās, gigantis (m) . . . . giant
7. grȳps, grȳphis (m) . . . . griffin
8. labyrinthus, -ī (m) . . . . labyrinth, maze
9. mīnōtaurus, -ī (m) . . . . minotaur
10. pēgasus, -ī (m) . . . . . pegasus
11. satyrus, -ī (m) . . . . . . satyr, faun

ADJECTIVES

12. ruber, -bra, -brum . . . red

VERBS

13. captō, captāre . . . . . . I hunt
14. commūnicō, commūnicāre . . I share, inform
15. nō, nāre . . . . I swim

Chant:

No new chant this week.

Quotation:

No quotation this week.

WEEK 22 *Derivatives:*

Weekly Worksheet 22

name: _____

A. Answer the following questions about commands.

1. When you tell a dog, "Fetch!", you're giving him a _____.

2. Is a command a noun, a verb, or an adjective? _____

3. Another word for "command" is _____.

4. To give a Latin command, you need to first find the verb's _____.

5. To give a singular command, what do you add to the stem? _____

6. To give a plural command using a first or second conjugation verb, what do you add to the stem? _____

7. How do you give a plural command using a third conjugation verb? _____
_____

B. Translate these singular commands into English.

1. Ede. _____   3. Commūnicā. _____

2. Respondē. _____   4. Nā! _____

Translate these plural commands into English.

5. Movetē! _____   7. Quiescite. _____

6. Commemorāte. _____   8. Cantāte! _____

C. Turn each verb into a singular command and a plural command in Latin. Then translate the plural command into English.

	VERB	SINGULAR COMMAND	PLURAL COMMAND	TRANSLATION
1.	vehō			

	VERB	SINGULAR COMMAND	PLURAL COMMAND	TRANSLATION
2.	portō			
3.	vibrō			
4.	dō			
5.	moneō			
6.	reptō			
7.	sedeō			
8.	mittō			

D. Translate these sentences into English. Some words will be review—feel free to use your dictionary!

1. Architectus rubrum dracōnem captābit. _____

2. Septem amīcī manent. _____

3. Volatne grӯps fessus? _____

4. Puerī quattuor nuntium commemorābunt. _____
_____

5. Equī decem stant. _____

6. Virgō rubrum fīlum crās dābit. _____

7. Candēlam habē. _____

8. Olefactāsne harēnam et pontum? _____

9. Gigantem improbum vulnerāte! _____

10. Erratne mīnōtaurus foedus semper? _____

11. Epistulae octō rēgem pacābunt. _____

12. Pābulum est bonum et caper parvus crescit. _____

E. Conjugate the following words in the present, future, and imperfect tenses.

Present Active

FIRST CONJUGATION

	SINGULAR	PLURAL
1ST	captō	
2ND		
3RD		

SECOND CONJUGATION

	SINGULAR	PLURAL
1ST	flōreō	
2ND		
3RD		

THIRD CONJUGATION

	SINGULAR	PLURAL
1ST	vehō	
2ND		
3RD		

Future Active

FIRST CONJUGATION

	SINGULAR	PLURAL
1ST		
2ND		
3RD		

SECOND CONJUGATION

	SINGULAR	PLURAL
1ST		
2ND		
3RD		

THIRD CONJUGATION

	SINGULAR	PLURAL
1ST		
2ND		
3RD		

Imperfect Active

FIRST CONJUGATION

	SINGULAR	PLURAL
1ST		
2ND		
3RD		

SECOND CONJUGATION

	SINGULAR	PLURAL
1ST		
2ND		
3RD		

THIRD CONJUGATION

	SINGULAR	PLURAL
1ST		
2ND		
3RD		

Latin Primer Book 2

G. Below is a *labyrinthus!* Help the baby *dracō* through it to find his mother.

WEEK 23

Word List

NOUNS

1. arcus, -ūs (m) . . . . bow, arch, rainbow
2. frūctus, -ūs (m) . . . . . . fruit, profit
3. lacus, -ūs (m) . . . . lake, tub, hollow
4. nix, nivis (f) . . . . snow
5. portus, -ūs (m) . . . . . . port, harbor
6. sōl, sōlis (m) . . . . sun
7. tellūs, tellūris (f) . . . . . earth, ground, land
8. umbra, -ae (f) . . . . shadow, shade
9. vīcus, -ī (m) . . . . village

ADJECTIVES

10. caldus, -a, -um . . . . . . warm, hot, fiery
11. novus, -a, -um . . . . . . new
12. opācus, -a, -um . . . . . dark, shaded

ADVERBS

13. clam . . . . secretly

VERBS

14. exspectō, exspectāre . . I wait, wait for, expect
15. foveō, fovēre . . . . I cherish, love, esteem

Chant:

Fourth Declension Noun Endings

	LATIN		ENGLISH	
	SINGULAR	PLURAL	SINGULAR	PLURAL
NOM.	-us	-ūs	a, the *noun*	the *nouns*
GEN.	-ūs	-uum	of the *noun*, the *noun's*	of the *nouns*, the *nouns'*
DAT.	-uī	-ibus	to, for the *noun*	to, for the *nouns*
ACC.	-um	-ūs	the *noun*	the *nouns*
ABL.	-ū	-ibus	by, with, from the *noun*	by, with, from the *nouns*

(Continued on the next page)

> **Quotation:**
> *albior super nivem*—"whiter than snow"

WEEK 23 *Derivatives:* _____

_____

Quotation: _____

Weekly Worksheet 23

name: _____

A. Complete the chant chart for this week and answer the questions about it.

	SINGULAR	PLURAL

1. Which case tells you a noun's declension? _____

2. The genitive singular ending for the fourth declension is _____.

3. The genitive singular ending for the third declension is _____.

4. The genitive singular ending for the second declension is _____.

5. The genitive singular ending for the first declension is _____.

B. Decline *arcus* and *frūctus* in the chart below and circle the nominative and accusative cases. Then answer the questions.

	SINGULAR	PLURAL
NOM.	arcus	
GEN.		
DAT.		
ACC.		
ABL.		

	SINGULAR	PLURAL
NOM.	frūctus	
GEN.		
DAT.		
ACC.		
ABL.		

Latin Primer Book 2

1. Which declension are *arcus* and *frūctus* in? _____

2. How can you tell? _____

C. For each noun, write in the blank whether it is in the first declension (1), second declension (2), second declension neuter (2N), third declension (3), third declension neuter (3N), or fourth declension (4).

1. cyclops, cyclōpis _____   6. corpus, corporis _____

2. satyrus, -ī _____   7. asinus, -ī _____

3. lacus, lacus _____   8. tībia, -ae _____

4. umbra, -ae _____   9. vulnus, vulneris _____

5. fīlum, -ī _____   10. portus, portus _____

D. Give the genitive singular form, gender (M, F, or N), declension, and the English translation for each noun.

	NOUN	GENITIVE	GENDER	DECLENSION	TRANSLATION
1.	tellūs				
2.	nix				
3.	centaurus				
4.	umbra				
5.	frūctus				
6.	vīcus				
7.	caput				
8.	arcus				

E. For each sentence, circle any subject nouns and underline any direct objects. Then translate the sentence into English.

1. Agricola tellūrem arābit. _____

2. Vīcum ferus vitābat. _____

3. Nix nova lūcet. _____

4. Centaurī bonī nuntiōs clam vehēbant. _____
_____

5. Hydrī ūmidī lacūs fovent. _____

6. Dux caldus nōn est opācus. _____

7. Arcum ūnā spectabamus. _____

8. Portābitisne habēnās et stimulōs? _____

9. Vīcus portūs novōs habet. _____

10. Datne tellūs frūctūs satis? _____

11. Cyclōpem exspectāte. _____

12. Umbrās opācās nōn timēmus. _____

F. Draw a line to match each derivative with its Latin root.

1. excruciating   caldus

2. gigantic   novus

3. cauldron   crux

4. filament   frūctus

5. albino   umbra

6. fructose   gigās

7. umbrella   albus

8. supernova   fīlum

G. Conjugate and translate *foveō* in the imperfect active tense.

Imperfect Active

LATIN

	SINGULAR	PLURAL
1ST		
2ND		
3RD		

ENGLISH

	SINGULAR	PLURAL
1ST		
2ND		
3RD		

H. Label each declension and complete the chants. Then circle all of the genitive endings.

_____ DECLENSION

	SINGULAR	PLURAL
NOM.		
GEN.	-ae	
DAT.		
ACC.		
ABL.		

_____ DECLENSION

	SINGULAR	PLURAL
NOM.		-ī
GEN.	-ī	
DAT.		
ACC.		
ABL.		

_____ DECLENSION _____

	SINGULAR	PLURAL
NOM.		-a
GEN.	-ī	
DAT.		
ACC.		
ABL.		

_____ DECLENSION

	SINGULAR	PLURAL
NOM.		-ēs
GEN.	-is	
DAT.		
ACC.		
ABL.		

_____ DECLENSION _____

	SINGULAR	PLURAL
NOM.		-a
GEN.	-is	
DAT.		
ACC.		
ABL.		

_____ DECLENSION

	SINGULAR	PLURAL
NOM.		
GEN.	-ūs	
DAT.		
ACC.		
ABL.		

WEEK 24

Word List

NOUNS

1. cantus, -ūs (m) . . . . . . song, singing
2. domus, -ūs (f) . . . . . . home, house
3. frāter, frātris (m) . . . . brother
4. Iesus, -ūs (m) . . . . . . Jesus
5. manus, -ūs (f) . . . . . . hand
6. māter, mātris (f) . . . . mother
7. metus, -ūs (m) . . . . . . fear, dread
8. pater, patris (m) . . . . . father
9. soror, sorōris (f) . . . . . sister
10. spīritus, -ūs (m) . . . . spirit, breath

ADJECTIVES

11. fīdus, -a, -um . . . . . . faithful, trustworthy

ADVERBS

12. repente . . . . suddenly

VERBS

13. appellō, appellāre . . . I name, call, call by name
14. commendō, commendāre . I commit, entrust
15. crēdō, crēdere . . . . . I believe

Chant:

No new chant this week.

Quotation:

Pater, in manūs tuās commendō spīritum meum.

"Father, into Your hands I commit my spirit." [Lk. 23:46]

WEEK 24 *Derivatives:*

Quotation:

Weekly Worksheet 24

name: _____

A. Match each genitive singular ending with its declension.

1. -is   first declension

2. -ī   second declension

3. -ae   third declension

4. -ūs   fourth declension

B. Label each noun's declension (1, 2, 3, or 4) and gender (M, F, or N). Then decline it.

DECLENSION _____ GENDER _____

	SINGULAR	PLURAL
NOM.	cantus	
GEN.		
DAT.		
ACC.		
ABL.		

DECLENSION _____ GENDER _____

	SINGULAR	PLURAL
NOM.	architectus	
GEN.		
DAT.		
ACC.		
ABL.		

DECLENSION _____ GENDER _____

	SINGULAR	PLURAL
NOM.	pater	
GEN.		
DAT.		
ACC.		
ABL.		

DECLENSION _____ GENDER _____

	SINGULAR	PLURAL
NOM.	metus	
GEN.		
DAT.		
ACC.		
ABL.		

C. Translate these sentences into English.

1. Pater et fīlius cervōs captābant. _____

2. Appellābatne māter sorōrem? _____

3. Sōl repente apparēbit. _____

4. Familia frātrem tardum exspectābat. _____

5. Vehēbāsne pēgasum? _____

6. Grȳphēs ālās magnās et brūnās pinnās habent. _____
_____

7. Iesus crucem portābat. _____

8. Māter et pater fābulam nōn crēdunt. _____
_____

9. Habetne lacus portum parvum? _____

10. Metūs minūtātim pacābō. _____

D. Turn each verb into a singular command and the plural command in Latin. Then translate the plural command into English.

	VERB	SINGULAR COMMAND	PLURAL COMMAND	TRANSLATION
1.	crēdō			
2.	edō			
3.	vibrō			
4.	appellō			
5.	foveō			

E. For each sentence, underline the verb and circle the subject. Then translate the sentence into Latin.

1. The father cherishes the land. _____

2. The brother was calling the sister. _____

3. The horrible cyclops will wait for the man. _____

4. Are you loving the song? _____

5. The minotaur has bad breath. _____

F. Each of the nouns below comes from a Latin root in either Word List 23 or 24. Figure out which of your Latin nouns is the root, and then give its English meaning.

	ITALIAN	SPANISH	FRENCH	LATIN	ENGLISH
1.	neve	nieve	neige		
2.	ombra	sombra	ombre		
3.	mano	mano	main		

G. Use your knowledge of Latin derivatives to circle the word that completes the definition.

1. *Maternal* love is the love of a _____.

   a) village   b) mother   c) sister   d) fear

2. *Solar* energy is energy from the _____.

   a) soul   b) moon   c) ground   d) sun

3. An *appellation* is a title or _____.

   a) name   b) rainbow   c) fruit   d) mountain

4. A *cauldron* is a pot that contains _____ liquids.

   a) colorful   b) delicious   c) hot   d) salty

H. Give the genitive forms of these nouns from memory and write whether they are in the first (1), second (2), second neuter (2N), third (3), third neuter (3N), or fourth (4) declension.

1. soror _____

2. sōl _____

3. vīcus _____

4. spīritus _____

5. manus _____

6. tellūs _____

7. pater _____

8. māter _____

I. Conjugate and translate *crēdō* in the present and imperfect active tenses.

Present Active

LATIN

	SINGULAR	PLURAL
1ST		
2ND		
3RD		

ENGLISH

	SINGULAR	PLURAL
1ST		
2ND		
3RD		

Imperfect Active

LATIN

	SINGULAR	PLURAL
1ST		
2ND		
3RD		

ENGLISH

	SINGULAR	PLURAL
1ST		
2ND		
3RD		

J. Write this week's quotation from Luke 23:46 in Latin.

_____

_____

Unit Four

Unit 4: Goals

By the end of Week 32, you should be able to . . .

- Recognize and decline any fourth declension noun
- Conjugate *possum* in the present tense
- Recognize and translate infinitives
- Conjugate *sum* in the present, future, and imperfect tenses

WEEK 25

Word List

NOUNS

1. cornū, -ūs (n) . . . . horn
2. culter, -trī (m) . . . . knife
4. gelū, -ūs (n) . . . . chill, frost
5. genū, -ūs (n) . . . . knee
6. grex, gregis (m) . . . . flock, herd
7. leō, leōnis (m) . . . . lion
8. pastor, pastōris (m) . . . . . shepherd
9. tempestās, tempestātis (f) . weather, storm
10. pecū, -ūs (n) . . . . cattle, flock
11. verū, -ūs (n) . . . . javelin, spit (for roasting meat)

ADJECTIVES

12. tūtus, -a, -um . . . . . . safe, secure

VERBS

13. cūrō, cūrāre . . . . I care for
14. terreō, terrēre . . . . . . I frighten, terrify
15. tondeō, tondēre . . . . I clip, give a haircut, shear
16. vigilō, vigilāre . . . . . . I guard, watch over

Chant:

Fourth Declension Neuter Noun Endings

	LATIN		ENGLISH	
	SINGULAR	PLURAL	SINGULAR	PLURAL
NOM.	-ū	-ua	a, the *noun*	the *nouns*
GEN.	-ūs	-uum	of the *noun*, the *noun's*	of the *nouns*, the *nouns'*
DAT.	-ū	-ibus	to, for the *noun*	to, for the *nouns*
ACC.	-ū	-ua	the *noun*	the *nouns*
ABL.	-ū	-ibus	by, with, from the *noun*	by, with, from the *nouns*

(Continued on the next page)

Latin Primer Book 2

> **Quotation:**
> *Dente lupus, cornū taurus petit.*
> "The wolf attacks with his fang, the bull with its horn."

WEEK 25 Derivatives: _____

_____

_____

_____

_____

_____

_____

_____

_____

_____

_____

_____

_____

_____

Quotation: _____

_____

_____

Weekly Worksheet 25

name: _____

A. Write the chant for this week and answer the questions about it.

	SINGULAR	PLURAL
NOM.		
GEN.		
DAT.		
ACC.		
ABL.		

1. Which case tells you a noun's declension? _____

2. The genitive singular ending for the fourth declension is _____.

3. How can you tell if a noun is in the fourth declension neuter? _____
_____

B. Decline *cornū* and *genū* in the chart below and circle the accusative endings. Then answer the questions.

	SINGULAR	PLURAL
NOM.	cornū	
GEN.		
DAT.		
ACC.		
ABL.		

	SINGULAR	PLURAL
NOM.	genū	
GEN.		
DAT.		
ACC.		
ABL.		

1. Which declension are *cornū* and *genū* in? _____

2. What is their gender? _____

Latin Primer Book 2

C. Give the genitive singular form, gender (M, F, or N), declension, and the English translation for each noun.

	NOUN	GENITIVE	GENDER	DECLENSION	TRANSLATION
1.	grex				
2.	culter				
3.	cantus				
4.	pecū				
5.	arcus				
6.	asinus				
7.	palma				
8.	gelū				
9.	fīlum				
10.	iter				

D. Underline the adjective that matches the noun's number, gender, and case. Then translate the phrase.

	NOUN	ADJECTIVE	TRANSLATION
1.	Pastor	fīdus / fīdum	
2.	Domūs	caldus / caldās	
3.	Gelū	mīrus / mīrum	
4.	Tellūs	opācus / opāca	
5.	Arcus	pulcher / pulchrōs	
6.	Matrimonia	beātum / beāta	
7.	Cornua	alba / albae	

E. Complete the chants. Then circle all of the accusative endings.

FIRST DECLENSION

	SINGULAR	PLURAL
NOM.	-a	
GEN.		
DAT.		
ACC.		
ABL.		

SECOND DECLENSION

	SINGULAR	PLURAL
NOM.	-us	
GEN.		
DAT.		
ACC.		
ABL.		

THIRD DECLENSION

	SINGULAR	PLURAL
NOM.	x	
GEN.		
DAT.		
ACC.		
ABL.		

F. Decline each of the nouns below.

	SINGULAR	PLURAL
NOM.	nōmen	
GEN.		
DAT.		
ACC.		
ABL.		

	SINGULAR	PLURAL
NOM.	portus	
GEN.		
DAT.		
ACC.		
ABL.		

	SINGULAR	PLURAL
NOM.	leō	
GEN.		
DAT.		
ACC.		
ABL.		

	SINGULAR	PLURAL
NOM.	fīlum	
GEN.		
DAT.		
ACC.		
ABL.		

G. Translate these sentences into English.

1. Pastor gregem fovet. _____

2. Tempestātem exspectābat. _____

3. Gregem tempestās terrēbit. _____

4. Pastor gregem vigilat et cūrat. _____

5. Grex est tūtus et nōn errābit. _____

6. Coquus verū vigilābat. _____

7. Soror frātrēs tondēbit. _____

8. Habetne leō cornua? _____

9. Genua sunt magna et ridicula. _____

10. Gelū gelidum ventum vehit. _____

H. Answer true (T) or false (F) for each statement about Latin sentences. The first one is done for you.

_____T_____ 1. The subject always takes the nominative case.

_____ 2. A command is a verb.

_____ 3. Direct objects take the accusative case.

_____ 4. Subject nouns must match a verb's gender.

_____ 5. To form a question, you can add -ne to the end of a verb.

_____ 6. A noun's genitive singular form tells you which conjugation it's in.

_____ 7. The accusative singular ending for the third declension is -em.

_____ 8. To find the base of a noun, you drop the genitive singular ending.

_____ 9. The stem of a verb is also a plural command.

_____ 10. *Terreō* is an "ā" family verb.

WEEK 26

Word List

NOUNS

1. arbor, arboris (f) . . . . . tree
2. fulmen, fulmenis (n) . . . lightning, thunderbolt
3. imber, imbris (m) . . . . . rain
4. lignum, -ī (n) . . . . wood, timber
5. lutum, -ī (n) . . . . mud
6. nūbēs, nūbis (f) . . . . . . cloud, gloom
7. rādix, rādīcis (f) . . . . . root
8. rāmus, -ī (m) . . . . branch, twig
9. tonitrus, -ūs (m) . . . . . thunder

ADVERBS

10. mox . . . . soon

VERBS

11. cadō, cadere . . . . I fall, sink, drop
12. flagrō, flagrāre . . . . . . I blaze, flame, burn
13. incendō, incendere . . . I kindle, set on fire
14. tangō, tangere . . . . . . I touch, strike
15. vastō, vastāre . . . . I devastate, lay waste

Chant:

No new chant this week.

> **Quotation:**
> *Frūctū cognoscitur arbor*—"The tree is known by its fruit"

WEEK 26 *Derivatives:*

Quotation:

Weekly Worksheet 26   name:

A. For each noun, write its declension and gender on the line above, then decline it.

DECLENSION _____ GENDER _____

	SINGULAR	PLURAL
NOM.	pecū	
GEN.		
DAT.		
ACC.		
ABL.		

DECLENSION _____ GENDER _____

	SINGULAR	PLURAL
NOM.	tonitrus	
GEN.		
DAT.		
ACC.		
ABL.		

DECLENSION _____ GENDER _____

	SINGULAR	PLURAL
NOM.	fulmen	
GEN.		
DAT.		
ACC.		
ABL.		

DECLENSION _____ GENDER _____

	SINGULAR	PLURAL
NOM.	genū	
GEN.		
DAT.		
ACC.		
ABL.		

B. Give the gender, case, and number of these nouns. Gender: masculine (M), feminine (F), or neuter (N). Case: nominative (NOM) or accusative (ACC). Number: singular (SG) or plural (PL). The first one is done for you.

1. tellūrem ___F___ACC___SG___

2. rādix _____

3. rāmum _____

4. portus _____

5. umbrās _____

6. tempestātem _____

7. leō _____

8. cornū _____ *or* _____

Latin Primer Book 2

C. Underline the adjective that matches the noun's number, gender, and case. Then translate the phrase.

NOUN	ADJECTIVE	TRANSLATION
1. Rādix	rubrum / rubra	_____
2. Nūbēs	opācās / opācus	_____
3. Ligna	ūmidum / ūmida	_____
4. Rāmī	nova / novī	_____
5. Tonitrus	foedus / foeda	_____
6. Manus	pulvereus / pulverea	_____
7. Verūa	antīquae / antīqua	_____
8. Arborem	firmum / firmam	_____

D. Conjugate each verb in the given tense.

Tondeō—Present Tense

LATIN

	SINGULAR	PLURAL
1ST		
2ND		
3RD		

ENGLISH

	SINGULAR	PLURAL
1ST		
2ND		
3RD		

Cadō—Future Tense

LATIN

	SINGULAR	PLURAL
1ST		
2ND		
3RD		

ENGLISH

	SINGULAR	PLURAL
1ST		
2ND		
3RD		

Vastō—Imperfect Tense

	LATIN		ENGLISH	
	SINGULAR	**PLURAL**	**SINGULAR**	**PLURAL**
1ST				
2ND				
3RD				

E. Translate these sentences into English.

1. Fulmen arborem antīquam incendit. _____

2. Tempestās gelida flōrēs vastat. _____

3. Cadentne imbrēs mox? _____

4. Cyclops gregem tondēbat. _____

5. Arbor rādicēs firmās crescēbat. _____

6. Leōnem videt et vītat. _____

7. Ligna flagrant et nivēs cadunt. _____

8. Pater mātrem fovet. _____

9. Timēbātisne tonitrum? _____

10. Nivēs frātrēs removēbant. _____

F. Pick a subject, verb, and direct object and write your own sentence, using the words from Weeks 25 and 26. Write it in English first, and then translate it into Latin.

Latin Primer Book 2

G. Label the *corpus* of the *leō* using the Latin terms below!

| crūs | nasus | caput | cauda | oculus | latus | coma |
| pēs | ōs | | | | | |

H. Use your knowledge of Latin to match the English derivatives on the left with their definitions on the right! Write the letter of the correct definition in the blank.

_____ 1. radish   a) a violent windstorm

_____ 2. florist   b) a waterfall

_____ 3. vigilant   c) watchful

_____ 4. tempest   d) a root vegetable

_____ 5. cascade   e) a person who grows or sells flowers

WEEK 27

Word List

NOUNS

1. carcer, carceris (m) . . . . prison
2. latrō, latrōnis (m) . . . . . robber
3. lēx, lēgis (f) . . . . law
4. mīles, mīlitis (m) . . . . . soldier
5. mūnus, mūneris (n) . . . duty, office
6. pecūnia, -ae (f) . . . . . . money
7. sepulcrum, -ī (n) . . . . . tomb, grave

ADJECTIVES

8. avārus, -a, -um . . . . . . greedy
9. ēgregius, -a, -um . . . . . outstanding

VERBS

10. caveō, cavēre . . . . . . I guard against, beware
11. dēbeō, dēbēre . . . . . . I owe, ought
12. iaceō, iacēre . . . . I lie down
13. mereō, merēre . . . . . I deserve, earn, am worthy of
14. possum, posse . . . . . I am able
15. quaerō, quaerere . . . . I search for, seek

Chant:

Possum, *I am able*—Present Active Irregular Verb

LATIN

	SINGULAR	PLURAL
1ST	possum	possumus
2ND	potes	potestis
3RD	potest	possunt

ENGLISH

	SINGULAR	PLURAL
1ST	I am able	we are able
2ND	you are able	you all are able
3RD	he/she/it is able	they are able

(Continued on the next page)

> **Quotation:**
> Tē audīre nōn possum —"I can't hear you"

WEEK 27 Derivatives:

Quotation:

Weekly Worksheet 27

name: _____

A. Answer the following questions.

1. In this week's Word List, *caveō* has two Latin forms. The first form, *caveō*, is called the _____ _____.

2. Does every verb have a first form? _____

3. Write the second form of *caveō* given in the Word List: _____

4. The second form of a verb is called the _____.

5. The second principal part is also called the _____.

6. Does every verb have a second principal part? _____

7. Give the second principal part of *quaerō:* _____

B. Translate the following infinitives into English. The first one is done for you.

1. iacēre   to lie down   6. tondēre _____

2. merēre _____   7. appellāre _____

3. dēbēre _____   8. tangere _____

4. cadere _____   9. retinēre _____

5. habēre _____   10. posse _____

C. Translate these infinitives into Latin.

1. to beware _____   5. to believe _____

2. to lay waste _____   6. to entrust _____

3. to care for _____   7. to trick _____

4. to watch over _____   8. to taste _____

D. Each of these short sentences uses an infinitive. First, find the main verb, then underline the infinitive, and translate the sentence. The first one is done for you.

1. Potes <u>iacēre</u>.   You are able to sleep.

2. Mereō edere. _____

3. Dēbēmus amāre. _____

4. Possum tondēre. _____

5. Dēbēs cavēre. _____

6. Potestis cantāre et exsultāre. _____

E. Write this week's chant in the box and translate it. Then answer the questions about it.

LATIN

	SINGULAR	PLURAL
1ST	possum	
2ND		
3RD		

ENGLISH

	SINGULAR	PLURAL
1ST		
2ND		
3RD		

1. Does *possum* conjugate regularly or irregularly? _____

2. Is this a chant of a complete verb or of verb endings? _____

F. Conjugate *dēbeō* in the present tense and translate it.

LATIN

	SINGULAR	PLURAL
1ST	dēbeō	
2ND		
3RD		

ENGLISH

	SINGULAR	PLURAL
1ST		
2ND		
3RD		

G. Give the stem of each verb, then write whether it is in the "ā" family (ā), "ē" family (ē), "e" family (e), or is irregular (IRR). Do not give a stem for irregular verbs.

1. flagrō, flagrāre _____
2. mereō, merēre _____
3. quaerō, quaerere _____
4. possum, posse _____
5. caveō, cavēre _____
6. incendō, incendere _____
7. nō, nāre _____
8. iaceō, iacēre _____
9. tangō, tangere _____
10. vastō, vastāre _____

H. For each noun, write its declension and gender on the line above, then decline it.

DECLENSION _____ GENDER _____

	SINGULAR	PLURAL
NOM.	mīles	
GEN.		
DAT.		
ACC.		
ABL.		

DECLENSION _____ GENDER _____

	SINGULAR	PLURAL
NOM.	sepulcrum	
GEN.		
DAT.		
ACC.		
ABL.		

DECLENSION _____ GENDER _____

	SINGULAR	PLURAL
NOM.	verū	
GEN.		
DAT.		
ACC.		
ABL.		

DECLENSION _____ GENDER _____

	SINGULAR	PLURAL
NOM.	mūnus	
GEN.		
DAT.		
ACC.		
ABL.		

I. Translate these sentences into English. Underline any infinitives.

1. Latrōnēs dēbent labōrāre. _____

2. Legātus mīlitem egregium commemorat. _____

3. Merētne regnāre? _____

4. Latrō carcerem intrābit. _____

5. Pastor ferum pācābat. _____

6. Non possum volāre. _____

7. Mīles legem dēbet commemorāre. _____

8. Sepulcra mīra quaerēmus. _____

9. Rēx grȳphem avārum cavet. _____

10. Agricolae agrōs properābunt arāre. _____

J. Use your knowledge of Latin derivatives to circle the word that completes the definition.

1. A *sepulcher* is a _____.

    a) skyscraper   b) ghost   c) tomb   d) village

2. *Avarice* is a _____ desire for money and wealth.

    a) natural   b) greedy   c) funny   d) kind

3. If someone is *incarcerated,* he is put in _____.

    a) oil   b) prison   c) space   d) a grave

4. An *insomniac* is a person who often cannot _____.

    a) sleep   b) sing   c) lie down   d) eat

WEEK 28

Word List

NOUNS

1. camēlus, -ī (m) . . . . camel
2. carō, carnis (f) . . . . meat, flesh
3. cȳgnus, -ī (m) . . . . swan
4. herba, -ae (f) . . . . herb, grass
5. hippopotāmus, -ī (m) . . . . . hippopotamus
6. hyaena, -ae (f) . . . . hyena
7. pardus, -ī (m) . . . . panther, leopard
8. psittācus, -ī (m) . . . . parrot
9. rhīnocerōs, rhīnocerōtis (m) . rhinoceros
10. serpēns, serpentis (m/f) . . . serpent, snake
11. sīmia, -ae (f) . . . . ape, monkey
12. ursa, -ae (f) *or* ursus, -ī (m) . bear

ADVERBS

13. numquam . . . . never

VERBS

14. domō, domāre . . . . I tame, subdue
15. mordeō, mordēre . . . . . . I bite, sting

Chant:
No new chant this week.

> **Quotation:**
> *prūdēns ut serpēns*—"wise as a serpent"

WEEK 28 *Derivatives:*

Quotation:

Weekly Worksheet 28

name: _____

A. For each noun, write its declension and gender on the line above, then decline it.

DECLENSION _____ GENDER _____

	SINGULAR	PLURAL
NOM.	pardus	
GEN.		
DAT.		
ACC.		
ABL.		

DECLENSION _____ GENDER _____

	SINGULAR	PLURAL
NOM.	carō	
GEN.		
DAT.		
ACC.		
ABL.		

DECLENSION _____ GENDER _____

	SINGULAR	PLURAL
NOM.	spīritus	
GEN.		
DAT.		
ACC.		
ABL.		

DECLENSION _____ GENDER _____

	SINGULAR	PLURAL
NOM.	sīmia	
GEN.		
DAT.		
ACC.		
ABL.		

B. Translate the following infinitives into English.

1. mordēre _____

2. peccāre _____

3. domāre _____

4. gaudēre _____

5. commendāre _____

6. hiemāre _____

7. repudiāre _____

8. cūrāre _____

C. Translate these infinitives into Latin.

1. to owe _____

2. to seek _____

3. to devastate _____

4. to fall _____

5. to lie down _____

6. to be able _____

D. Conjugate *mordeō* in the present, future, and imperfect tenses.

Present Tense

LATIN

	SINGULAR	PLURAL
1ST		
2ND		
3RD		

ENGLISH

	SINGULAR	PLURAL

Future Tense

LATIN

	SINGULAR	PLURAL
1ST		
2ND		
3RD		

ENGLISH

	SINGULAR	PLURAL

Imperfect Tense

LATIN

	SINGULAR	PLURAL
1ST		
2ND		
3RD		

ENGLISH

	SINGULAR	PLURAL

E. Translate these sentences into Latin.

1. The woman was taming a blue parrot. _____

2. Do you see the yellow dragon? _____

3. The swans are not able to bite. _____

4. Always beware! (plural) _____

F. On the lines below, give the Latin word for each zoo animal!

1. _____ 2. _____ 3. _____ 4. _____

5. _____ 6. _____ 7. _____ 8. _____

G. Translate these sentences into English.

1. Cȳgnī et psittācī possunt volāre. _____

2. Mīlites sepulchrum vigilābant. _____

3. Numquam mordē! _____

4. Frāter camēlum vehēbat. _____

5. Homō caecus lūcem nōn potest vidēre. _____

6. Intratne lūx carcerem? _____

7. Hyaenae improbae rident. _____

8. Rēx avārus pecūniam amat. _____

9. Rhīnocerōtem mox domābō! _____

10. Potesne nāre? _____

H. Underline the adjective that matches the noun's number, gender, and case. Then translate the phrase.

NOUN	ADJECTIVE	TRANSLATION
1. Herba	ēgregiās / ēgregia	
2. Sepulcra	album / alba	
3. Pardōs	maculōsa / maculōsōs	
4. Serpēns	pulcher / pulchram	
5. Carō	dēliciōsus / dēliciōsa	
6. Sīmiae	rīdiculae / rīdicula	
7. Mīlitēs	fessus / fessī	
8. Dracō	caldō / caldus	

I. Fill in the blank by writing the noun in the correct case.

1. "flesh" in the genitive singular _____

2. "trees" in the accusative plural _____

3. "snakes" in the nominative plural _____

4. "swan" in the accusative singular _____

WEEK 29

Word List

NOUNS

1. aestās, aestātis (f) . . . . summer
2. Carthāgō, Carthāginis (f) . . . Carthage
3. Eurōpa, -ae (f) . . . . . . Europe
4. fīnitimus, -ī (m) . . . . . neighbor
5. Gallia, -ae (f) . . . . Gaul
6. hiems, hiemis (f) . . . . . winter, bad weather
7. homō, hominis (m) . . . . man, human being
8. Ītalia, -ae (f) . . . . Italy
9. Rōma, -ae (f) . . . . Rome
10. terminus, -ī (m) . . . . . end, boundary, limit

ADJECTIVES

11. celsus, -a, -um . . . . . . tall, high, lofty

ADVERBS

12. undique . . . . on/from all sides, from every direction

VERBS

13. vexō, vexāre . . . . I annoy, harass
14. vītō, vītāre . . . . I avoid

Chant:

No new chant this week.

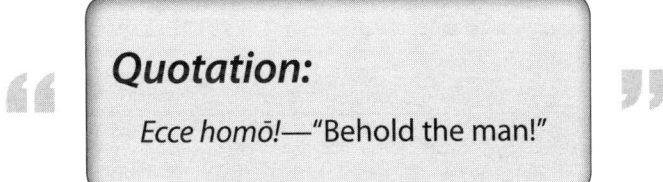

Quotation:

Ecce homō!—"Behold the man!"

WEEK 29 *Derivatives:*

Quotation:

Weekly Worksheet 29

name: _____

A. Fill in the blanks.

1. The _____ case is used for direct objects.

2. A *direct object* receives the action of the _____.

3. A *verb* expresses _____ or a state of _____.

4. The part of speech that *renames or identifies the subject* is called the _____ _____.

5. Which Latin case do you use for this part of speech? _____

6. Which Latin case do you use for the subject? _____

B. List each noun's gender, declension, and its nominative plural form. The first one is done for you.

	NOUN	GENDER	DECLENSION	NOMINATIVE PLURAL
1.	terminus	M	2	terminī
2.	hiems			
3.	fīnitimus			
4.	ursa			
5.	aestās			
6.	carō			
7.	homō			
8.	sepulcrum			
9.	mūnus			
10.	Gallia			

C. Circle all the *being verbs* below.

| move | are | frighten | show | is | avoid |
| am | increase | teach | will be | sniff | was |

D. Conjugate and translate *sum* in the present and future tenses.

Present Tense

LATIN

	SINGULAR	PLURAL
1ST		
2ND		
3RD		

ENGLISH

	SINGULAR	PLURAL
1ST		
2ND		
3RD		

Future Tense

LATIN

	SINGULAR	PLURAL
1ST		
2ND		
3RD		

ENGLISH

	SINGULAR	PLURAL
1ST		
2ND		
3RD		

E. In each English sentence, underline subject nouns and circle predicate nouns. If there is a predicate noun, translate it into Latin and write it in the blank. (Hint: Remember which case the predicate noun takes!) The first one is done for you.

1. A wolf is a wild animal. _____ferus_____

2. Little Red Riding Hood was a girl. _____

3. It will not always be summer. _____

4. One of the four seasons is winter. _____

5. Princess Aurora will be the queen. _____

6. The wicked witch was her enemy. _____

7. Turkey, bacon, and ham are all meats. _____

8. My favorite city in all the world is Rome. _____

9. Coco is the name of our parrot. _____

F. For each sentence, first find the verb. Once you've found it, underline the subject and circle the predicate noun. Then translate the sentence into English.

1. Fīlius est agricola. _____

2. Frātrēs sunt latrōnēs. _____

3. Pastor nōn est nauta. _____

4. Hominēs sunt fīnitimī. _____

5. Nōn sumus gigantēs. _____

G. Label the parts of each sentence: S for subject, V for verb, DO for direct object, and PN for predicate noun. Then translate the sentence into English.

1. Muscae equum undique vexant. _____

2. Fīlia est rēgīna. _____

3. Portābisne pulvīnōs rubrōs? _____

4. Hominēs sunt legātī. _____

5. Colōnī celsī sunt agricolae. _____

6. Taurus ferus campum vastābit. _____

7. Pecū umbram videt. _____

8. Sumus discipulī rīdiculī. _____

9. Esne coquus? _____

10. Fluvius erit terminus. _____

F. Use a map, an encyclopedia, or the internet to find the following places and label them below.

    Carthāgō   Gallia   Ītalia   Rōma

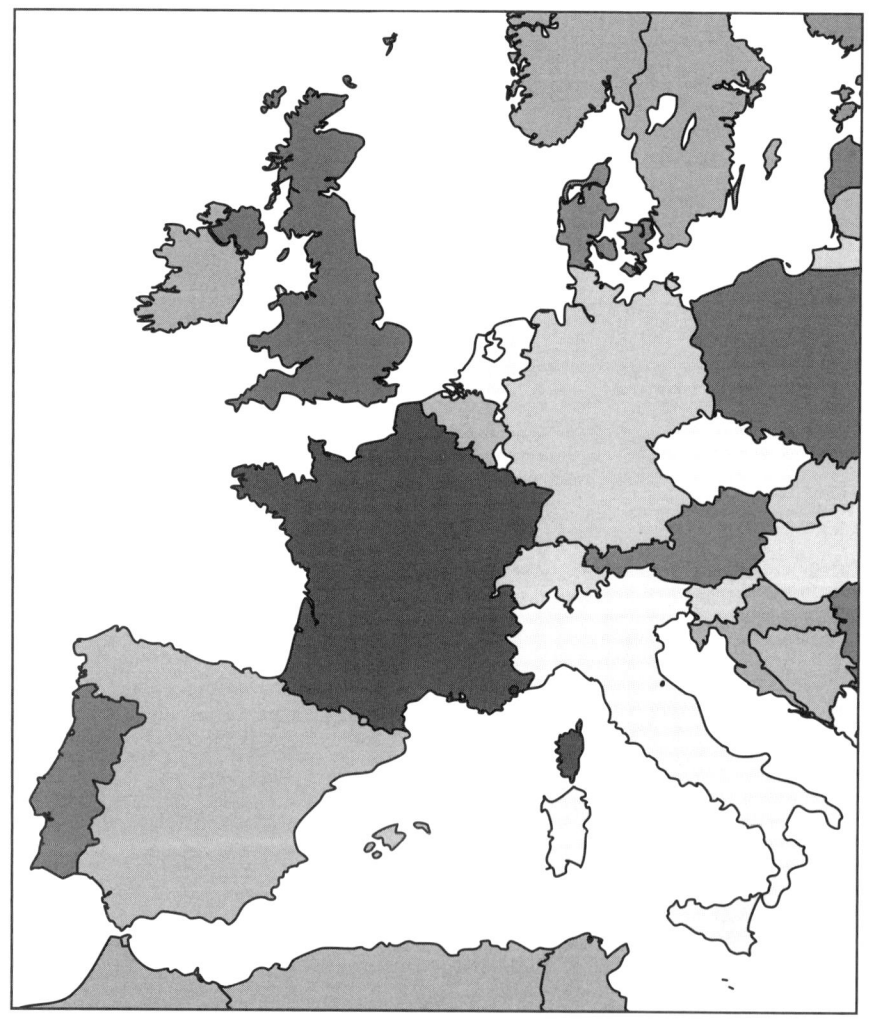

WEEK 30

Word List

NOUNS

1. būtūrum, -ī (n) . . . . . . butter
2. crūstulum, -ī (n) . . . . . cookie, small cake
3. farīna, -ae (f) . . . . flour
4. lāc, lactis (n) . . . . milk
5. ōvum, -ī (n) . . . . egg
6. patella, -ae (f) . . . . . . plate, dish
7. pōculum, -ī (n) . . . . . . cup
8. sacchārum, -ī (n) . . . . . sugar

CONJUGATIONS

9. sīve . . . . or

VERBS

10. bibō, bibere . . . . I drink
11. consecō, consecāre . . . I chop, cut up
12. coquō, coquere . . . . . I cook, bake
13. emō, emere . . . . I buy, purchase
14. eram . . . . I was
15. frangō, frangere . . . . I break

Chant:

Eram, *I was*—Imperfect Active of *Sum*
Irregular Verb

LATIN

	SINGULAR	PLURAL
1ST	eram	erāmus
2ND	erās	erātis
3RD	erat	erant

ENGLISH

	SINGULAR	PLURAL
1ST	I was	we were
2ND	you were	you all were
3RD	he/she/it was	they were

> **Quotation:**
> *Mihine crūstula coquēs?*—"Will you bake cookies for me?"

WEEK 30 *Derivatives:*

Quotation:

Weekly Worksheet 30

name: _____

A. Conjugate *sum* in the imperfect tense and translate it. Then answer the questions about it.

LATIN

	SINGULAR	PLURAL
1ST	eram	
2ND		
3RD		

ENGLISH

	SINGULAR	PLURAL
1ST		
2ND		
3RD		

1. Is *eram* a regular or irregular verb? _____

2. Is *eram* an action verb or a being verb? _____

B. For each noun, write its declension and gender on the line above. Then decline each noun by adding the endings to the base that is given. Each noun's nominative and genitive singular forms are provided.

DECLENSION _____ GENDER _____

	SINGULAR	PLURAL
NOM.	būtūrum	būtūr
GEN.	būtūrī	būtūr
DAT.	būtūr	būtūr
ACC.	būtūr	būtūr
ABL.	būtūr	būtūr

DECLENSION _____ GENDER _____

	SINGULAR	PLURAL
NOM.	lāc	lact
GEN.	lactis	lact
DAT.	lact	lact
ACC.	lac	lact
ABL.	lact	lact

C. In each English sentence, underline the subject and circle the predicate noun. Then translate the predicate noun into Latin and write it in the blank. (Hint: Remember which case the predicate noun takes!)

1. The first ingredient is butter. _____

2. Her surprise was a small cake. _____

3. That bird is a swan. _____

4. Italy is a neighbor to Gaul. _____

5. A birch is a tree. _____

D. Fill in the blanks.

1. The _____ case is used for direct objects.

2. A *direct object* receives the action of the _____.

3. A *verb* expresses _____ or _____ .

4. The part of speech that *renames or identifies the subject* is called the _____ _____.

5. Which Latin case do you use for this part of speech? _____

E. Label the parts of each sentence: S for subject, V for main verb, DO for direct object, and PN for predicate noun. Then translate the sentence into English.

1. Coquus ōva quattuor frangit. _____

2. Frāter est fīnitimus. _____

3. Crūstula dēliciōsa amō coquere! _____

4. Ursī sunt ferī. _____

5. Dux Eurōpam nōn potest vastāre. _____

6. Carthāginem copiae undique vexābant. _____

7. Emēsne farīnam, lacte, sīve sacchārum? _____

8. Mīles ligna consecābat. _____

F. Each of the nouns below comes from a Latin root in either Word List 29 or 30. Figure out which of your Latin nouns is the root, and then give its English meaning.

	ITALIAN	SPANISH	FRENCH	LATIN	ENGLISH
1.	uomo	hombre	homme		
2.	latte	leche	lait		
3.	farina	harina	farine		

G. Conjugate and translate *bibō* in the present, future, and imperfect tenses.

Present Tense

LATIN

	SINGULAR	PLURAL
1ST		
2ND		
3RD		

ENGLISH

	SINGULAR	PLURAL
1ST		
2ND		
3RD		

Future Tense

LATIN

	SINGULAR	PLURAL
1ST		
2ND		
3RD		

ENGLISH

	SINGULAR	PLURAL
1ST		
2ND		
3RD		

Latin Primer Book 2

Imperfect Tense

LATIN

	SINGULAR	PLURAL
1ST		
2ND		
3RD		

ENGLISH

	SINGULAR	PLURAL
1ST		
2ND		
3RD		

H. Below are *direct object* nouns. Underline the adjective that matches each noun's number, gender, and case. Then translate the phrase.

NOUN	ADJECTIVE	TRANSLATION
1. Farīnam	albās / albam	
2. Būtūrum	flavus / flavum	
3. Carthāginem	antīquus / antīquum	
4. Rāmum	celsus / celsum	
5. Patellās	pulchrīs / pulchrās	
6. Cornū	maculōsum / maculōsōs	
7. Cantūs	laetum / laetōs	
8. Gregēs	tūtum / tūtōs	
9. Camēlōs	avārōs / avārās	
10. Aestātem	ēgregiam / ēgregium	

I. Answer the following questions about your Latin quotations.

1. Translate *Mihine crūstula coquēs?* into English. _____

2. Which Latin word is the verb? _____

3. Is the verb in the "ā" family, the "ē" family, or the "e" family? _____

4. What Latin ending tells you that this is a question? _____

WEEK 31

Word List

NOUNS

1. Brittania, -ae (f) . . . . . Britain
2. eques, equitis (m) . . . . horseman, knight
3. exercitus, -ūs (m) . . . . . army
4. Germānia, -ae (f) . . . . . Germany
5. Hispānia, -ae (f) . . . . . . Spain
6. regnum, -ī (n) . . . . kingdom
7. tuba, -ae (f) . . . . trumpet
8. vadum, -ī (n) . . . . ford, shallows

ADJECTIVES

9. extrēmus, -a, -um . . . . last, farthest, outermost
10. longinquus, -a, -um . . far away, distant

ADVERBS

11. quondam . . . . once, formerly

VERBS

12. equitō, equitāre . . . . . I ride (horseback)
13. habitō, habitāre . . . . . I live in, dwell, inhabit

Chant:
No new chant this week.

> **Quotation:**
>
> *eques ipso melior Bellerophonte*
>
> "A better horseman than Bellerophon himself"

WEEK 31 *Derivatives:*

Quotation:

Weekly Worksheet 31

name: _____

A. Answer the following questions about this week's Word List.

1. What are the two second declension nouns in this week's Word List? _____

   _____

2. What is their gender? _____

3. *Exercitus* and *lacus* look like second declension nouns. What tells you that they are not? _____

   _____

B. Write each Latin word in the given form.

1. *latrō* in accusative singular _____

2. *exercitus* in accusative singular _____

3. *mūrus* in accusative singular _____

4. *tuba* in accusative singular _____

5. *puella* in accusative plural _____

6. *regnum* in nominative plural _____

7. *vīcus* in nominative plural _____

8. *tellūs* in nominative plural _____

C. Conjugate and translate *eram*. Then answer the questions about it.

LATIN

	SINGULAR	PLURAL
1ST	eram	
2ND		
3RD		

ENGLISH

	SINGULAR	PLURAL
1ST		
2ND		
3RD		

D. Give the masculine, feminine, and neuter *accusative plural* forms of these adjectives in Latin.

	ADJECTIVE	MASCULINE	FEMININE	NEUTER
1.	last			
2.	distant			
3.	sunny			

E. Label each noun's declension (1, 2, or 3) and gender (M, F, or N). Then decline it.

DECLENSION _____ GENDER _____

	SINGULAR	PLURAL
NOM.		
GEN.	equitis	
DAT.		
ACC.		
ABL.		

DECLENSION _____ GENDER _____

	SINGULAR	PLURAL
NOM.		
GEN.	exercitūs	
DAT.		
ACC.		
ABL.		

F. Translate these sentences into English.

1. Exercitūs Brittaniam vexābant undique. _____

2. Brittania est īnsula. _____

3. Estne Brittania īnsula parva? _____

4. Agricola mūrum removēbit. _____

5. Mīles salsus est poēta. _____

6. Bovem quondam equitabam! _____

7. Rēgīna Hispāniam longinquam habitāt. _____

_____

8. Equus fīdus stabulum astābat. _____

9. Latrō quondam erat eques mīrus. _____

10. Carthāgō erat regnum antīquum. _____

G. Use a map, an encyclopedia, or the internet to find the following places and label them below.

Brittania   Carthāgō   Gallia   Germānia   Hispānia   Ītalia   Rōma

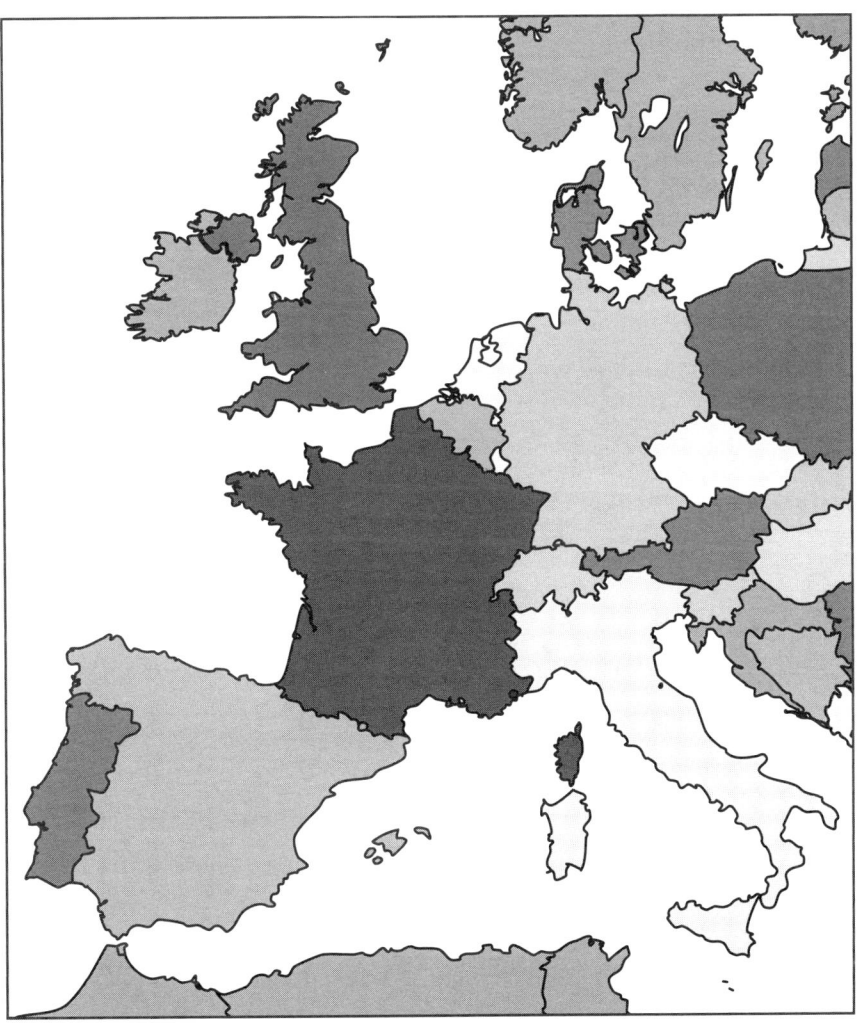

Latin Primer Book 2

H. Translate these commands into English.

1. Amīcum astā. _____

2. Pecūniam nōn amāte. _____

3. Arā terram. _____

4. Vītā hominēs improbōs. _____

5. Occultā librum statim! _____

I. Underline the predicate nouns in these sentences, then translate the sentence into Latin.

1. The letter was a complaint. _____

2. Britain and Spain are kingdoms. _____

3. The men will be outstanding knights. _____

4. The girl will be a teacher. _____

5. The fruits were strawberries and bananas. _____

J. Find and circle the hidden vocabulary words!

| vadum | eram | sive | psittacus | regnum | bibo |
| tuba | extremus | emo | Germania | undique | quondam |

```
m a r b i b o q e s i v e
r e g n u m u k l g o e p
y o e w a v p c a e f r s
u j x b e a l w u r e a i
n d t n k d t h e m o m t
d h r l t u b a k a o x t
i v e p y m k x u n j h a
q c m g d t f w i i y z c
u q u o n d a m p a r t u
e s s c r w i t r s m o s
```

WEEK 32

Word List

VERBS

1. dīrigō, dīrigere . . . . . . I direct
2. pōnō, pōnere . . . . I put, place
3. praedīcō, pradīcere . . . I proclaim
4. vincō, vincere . . . . I conquer

Chant:

No new chant this week.

Quotation:

No new quotation this week.

WEEK 32 *Derivatives:*

Weekly Worksheet 32

name: _____

A. Conjugate the following words in the present, future, and imperfect tenses.

Present Active

FIRST CONJUGATION

	SINGULAR	PLURAL
1ST	domō	
2ND		
3RD		

SECOND CONJUGATION

	SINGULAR	PLURAL
1ST	caveō	
2ND		
3RD		

THIRD CONJUGATION

	SINGULAR	PLURAL
1ST	pōnō	
2ND		
3RD		

Future Active

FIRST CONJUGATION

	SINGULAR	PLURAL
1ST		
2ND		
3RD		

SECOND CONJUGATION

	SINGULAR	PLURAL
1ST		
2ND		
3RD		

THIRD CONJUGATION

	SINGULAR	PLURAL
1ST		
2ND		
3RD		

Imperfect Active

FIRST CONJUGATION

	SINGULAR	PLURAL
1ST		
2ND		
3RD		

SECOND CONJUGATION

	SINGULAR	PLURAL
1ST		
2ND		
3RD		

THIRD CONJUGATION

	SINGULAR	PLURAL
1ST		
2ND		
3RD		

B. Give the function (subject, direct object, predicate noun), case, number, and Latin form of each underlined noun. The first one is done for you.

1. The dove's <u>wing</u> is broken.   subject, nominative, singular, *āla*

2. The sailor does not see the wave. _____

3. The clouds hide the sun. _____

4. The farmer is a settler. _____

5. A rabbit is approaching the hiding place. _____

6. Those neighbors are brothers. _____

7. The horse carries the master. _____

8. The horse is avoiding the spurs. _____

9. Suddenly the archer sees a deer. _____

10. The boy is a poet. _____

11. The woman will save the sons. _____

C. Draw a line to match each derivative with its Latin root.

1. dirigible	coquō
2. saccharine	vadum
3. invincible	extrēmus
4. butter	dīrigō
5. cook	praedīcō
6. wade	sacchārum
7. fragile	habitō
8. extremity	vincō
9. habitat	frangō
10. predict	būtūrum

D. For each noun, give its declension and gender, then decline it.

DECLENSION _____ GENDER _____

	SINGULAR	PLURAL
NOM.	exercitus	
GEN.		
DAT.		
ACC.		
ABL.		

DECLENSION _____ GENDER _____

	SINGULAR	PLURAL
NOM.	pōculum	
GEN.		
DAT.		
ACC.		
ABL.		

DECLENSION _____ GENDER _____

	SINGULAR	PLURAL
NOM.	tuba	
GEN.		
DAT.		
ACC.		
ABL.		

DECLENSION _____ GENDER _____

	SINGULAR	PLURAL
NOM.	lāc	
GEN.		
DAT.		
ACC.		
ABL.		

DECLENSION _____ GENDER _____

	SINGULAR	PLURAL
NOM.	cȳgnus	
GEN.		
DAT.		
ACC.		
ABL.		

DECLENSION _____ GENDER _____

	SINGULAR	PLURAL
NOM.	domus	
GEN.		
DAT.		
ACC.		
ABL.		

DECLENSION _____ GENDER _____

	SINGULAR	PLURAL
NOM.	aestās	
GEN.		
DAT.		
ACC.		
ABL.		

DECLENSION _____ GENDER _____

	SINGULAR	PLURAL
NOM.	verū	
GEN.		
DAT.		
ACC.		
ABL.		

E. Fill in the blanks.

1. The _____ case is used for direct objects.

2. A *direct object* receives the action of the _____ .

3. A *verb* expresses _____ or _____ .

4. The part of speech that *renames or identifies the subject* is called the _____ _____ .

5. Which Latin case do you use for this part of speech? _____

6. Which Latin case do you use for the subject? _____

F. Underline the adjective that matches the noun's number, gender, and case. Then translate the phrase.

NOUN	ADJECTIVE	TRANSLATION
1. Cunīculus	albus / albōs	_____
2. Rēgīna	ruber / rubra	_____
3. Regna	extrēmum / extrēma	_____
4. Lacūs	opācus / opācī	_____
5. Gigās	salsus / salsās	_____

6. Hominem   bonum / bonōrum   _____

7. Arbor   celsus / celsa   _____

8. Equitēs   honestum / honestī   _____

G. Give the stem of each verb and which conjugation it's in. The first one is done for you.

	VERB	STEM	CONJUGATION
1.	vigilō, vigilāre	vigilā-	1
2.	mordeō, mordēre		
3.	equitō, equitāre		
4.	praedīcō, pradīcere		
5.	vītō, vītāre		
6.	tangō, tangere		
7.	caveō, cavēre		
8.	vincō, vincere		

H. Translate these sentences into English.

1. Gallia erat provincia antīqua. _____

2. Parva puella fungum edēbat. _____

3. Dux vadum significat. _____

4. Lacus nunc est serēnus. _____

5. Lacus nōn erat serēnus herī. _____

6. Pontus erat longinquus. _____

7. Tuba tardum exercitum dīriget. _____

8. Edisne crūstulum sīve mālum? _____

9. Spēluncae erunt latebrae bonae. _____

10. Metum amō vincere. _____

I. In each sentence, first find the main verb. Then underline subjects, circle direct objects, and draw a box around predicate nouns. Finally, translate each sentence into Latin.

1. The soldier is a giant. _____

2. The knights are friends. _____

3. The robber was avoiding the province. _____

4. The sea was the boundary. _____

5. Rome is not often conquered. _____

6. The free towns will change the law. _____

7. The brother is not able to avoid the neighbors. _____
_____

8. The boys will be good apprentices. _____

9. Did you all see a horrible griffin? _____

10. Proclaim the story! _____

J. On the lines below, label what each animal is called in Latin.

1. _____   2. _____   3. _____   4. _____

Appendices

- Chant Charts
- Glossary
- Sources and Helps

CHANT CHARTS

Chants, in Order of Introduction

The chants in this section are listed in the order they are introduced in this book.

First Declension Noun Endings (Week 1, p. 5)

	SINGULAR	PLURAL	SINGULAR	PLURAL
NOM.	-a	-ae	a, the *noun*	the *nouns*
GEN.	-ae	-ārum	of the *noun*, the *noun's*	of the *nouns*, the *nouns'*
DAT.	-ae	-īs	to, for the *noun*	to, for the *nouns*
ACC.	-am	-ās	the *noun*	the *nouns*
ABL.	-ā	-īs	by, with, from the *noun*	by, with, from the *nouns*

Second Declension Noun Endings (Week 2, p. 11)

	SINGULAR	PLURAL	SINGULAR	PLURAL
NOM.	-us	-ī	a, the *noun*	the *nouns*
GEN.	-ī	-ōrum	of the *noun*, the *noun's*	of the *nouns*, the *nouns'*
DAT.	-ō	-īs	to, for the *noun*	to, for the *nouns*
ACC.	-um	-ōs	the *noun*	the *nouns*
ABL.	-ō	-īs	by, with, from the *noun*	by, with, from the *nouns*

Second Declension Neuter Noun Endings (Week 3, p. 17)

	SINGULAR	PLURAL	SINGULAR	PLURAL
NOM.	-um	-a	a, the *noun*	the *nouns*
GEN.	-ī	-ōrum	of the *noun*, the *noun's*	of the *nouns*, the *nouns'*
DAT.	-ō	-īs	to, for the *noun*	to, for the *nouns*
ACC.	-um	-a	the *noun*	the *nouns*
ABL.	-ō	-īs	by, with, from the *noun*	by, with, from the *nouns*

Present Active Verb Endings
(Week 4, p. 23)

	SINGULAR	PLURAL		SINGULAR	PLURAL
1ST	-ō	-mus		I am *verbing*, I *verb*	we are *verbing*
2ND	-s	-tis		you are *verbing*	you all are *verbing*
3RD	-t	-nt		he/she/it is *verbing*	they are *verbing*

Future Active Verb Endings
(Week 5, p. 29)

	SINGULAR	PLURAL		SINGULAR	PLURAL
1ST	-bō	-bimus		I will *verb*	we will *verb*
2ND	-bis	-bitis		you will *verb*	you all will *verb*
3RD	-bit	-bunt		he/she/it will *verb*	they will *verb*

Imperfect Active Verb Endings
(Week 6, p. 35)

	SINGULAR	PLURAL		SINGULAR	PLURAL
1ST	-bam	-bāmus		I was *verbing*	we were *verbing*
2ND	-bās	-bātis		you were *verbing*	you all were *verbing*
3RD	-bat	-bant		he/she/it was *verbing*	they were *verbing*

Dūcō, *I lead*—Present Active
Third Conjugation or "e" Family Verb
(Week 9, p. 55)

	SINGULAR	PLURAL		SINGULAR	PLURAL
1ST	dūcō	dūcimus		I lead	we lead
2ND	dūcis	dūcitis		you lead	you all lead
3RD	dūcit	dūcunt		he/she/it leads	they lead

Sum, *I am*—Present Active
Irregular Verb
(Week 10, p. 61)

	SINGULAR	PLURAL		SINGULAR	PLURAL
1ST	sum	sumus		I am	we are
2ND	es	estis		you are	you all are
3RD	est	sunt		he/she/it is	they are

Dūcam, *I will lead*—Future Active
Third Conjugation or "e" Family Verb
(Week 11, p. 67)

	SINGULAR	PLURAL	SINGULAR	PLURAL
1ST	dūcam	dūcēmus	I will lead	we will lead
2ND	dūcēs	dūcētis	you will lead	you all will lead
3RD	dūcet	dūcent	he/she/it will lead	they will lead

Dūcēbam, *I was leading*—Imperfect Active
Third Conjugation or "e" Family Verb Endings
(Week 12, p. 73)

	SINGULAR	PLURAL	SINGULAR	PLURAL
1ST	dūcēbam	dūcēbāmus	I was leading	we were leading
2ND	dūcēbās	dūcēbātis	you were leading	you all were leading
3RD	dūcēbat	dūcēbant	he/she/it was leading	they were leading

Third Declension Noun Endings
(Week 13, p. 79)

	SINGULAR	PLURAL	SINGULAR	PLURAL
NOM.	x	-ēs	a, the *noun*	the *nouns*
GEN.	-is	-um	of the *noun*, the *noun's*	of the *nouns*, the *nouns'*
DAT.	-ī	-ibus	to, for the *noun*	to, for the *nouns*
ACC.	-em	-ēs	the *noun*	the *nouns*
ABL.	-e	-ibus	by, with, from the *noun*	by, with, from the *nouns*

Third Declension Neuter Noun Endings
(Week 15, p. 91)

	SINGULAR	PLURAL	SINGULAR	PLURAL
NOM.	x	-a	a, the *noun*	the *nouns*
GEN.	-is	-um	of the *noun*, the *noun's*	of the *nouns*, the *nouns'*
DAT.	-ī	-ibus	to, for the *noun*	to, for the *nouns*
ACC.	x	-a	the *noun*	the *nouns*
ABL.	-e	-ibus	by, with, from the *noun*	by, with, from the *nouns*

Erō, *I will be*—Future Active of *Sum*
Irregular Verb (Week 16, p. 97)

	SINGULAR	PLURAL	SINGULAR	PLURAL
1ST	erō	erimus	I will be	we will be
2ND	eris	eritis	you will be	you all will be
3RD	erit	erunt	he/she/it will be	they will be

Fourth Declension Noun Endings (Week 23, p. 141)

	SINGULAR	PLURAL	SINGULAR	PLURAL
NOM.	-us	-ūs	a, the *noun*	the *nouns*
GEN.	-ūs	-uum	of the *noun*, the *noun's*	of the *nouns*, the *nouns'*
DAT.	-uī	-ibus	to, for the *noun*	to, for the *nouns*
ACC.	-um	-ūs	the *noun*	the *nouns*
ABL.	-ū	-ibus	by, with, from the *noun*	by, with, from the *nouns*

Fourth Declension Neuter Noun Endings (Week 25, p. 155)

	SINGULAR	PLURAL	SINGULAR	PLURAL
NOM.	-ū	-ua	a, the *noun*	the *nouns*
GEN.	-ūs	-uum	of the *noun*, the *noun's*	of the *nouns*, the *nouns'*
DAT.	-ū	-ibus	to, for the *noun*	to, for the *nouns*
ACC.	-ū	-ua	the *noun*	the *nouns*
ABL.	-ū	-ibus	by, with, from the *noun*	by, with, from the *nouns*

Possum, *I am able*—Present Active
Irregular Verb (Week 27, p. 167)

	SINGULAR	PLURAL	SINGULAR	PLURAL
1ST	possum	possumus	I am able	we are able
2ND	potes	potestis	you are able	you all are able
3RD	potest	possunt	he/she/it is able	they are able

Eram, *I was*—Imperfect Active of *Sum*
Irregular Verb

(Week 30, p. 185)

	SINGULAR	PLURAL	SINGULAR	PLURAL
1ST	eram	erāmus	I was	we were
2ND	erās	erātis	you were	you all were
3RD	erat	erant	he/she/it was	they were

Verb Chants, applied to Amō, Videō, and Dūcō

The chants in this section follow the conjugations of amō (1st), videō (2nd), and dūcō (3rd). The notation [PV] stands for "passive voice." Conjugations without this notation are in the active voice.

LATIN	SINGULAR			PLURAL		
	1ST	2ND	3RD	1ST	2ND	3RD
PRESENT	amō	amās	amat	amāmus	amātis	amant
FUTURE	amābō	amābis	amābit	amābimus	amābitis	amābunt
IMPERFECT	amābam	amābās	amābat	amābāmus	amābātis	amābant
PERFECT	amāvī	amāvistī	amāvit	amāvimus	amāvistis	amāvērunt
FUTURE PERFECT	amāverō	amāveris	amāverit	amāverimus	amāveritis	amāverint
PLUPERFECT	amāveram	amāverās	amāverat	amāverāmus	amāverātis	amāverant
PRESENT [PV]	amor	amāris	amātur	amāmur	amāminī	amantur
FUTURE [PV]	amābor	amāberis	amābitur	amābimur	amābiminī	amābuntur
IMPERFECT [PV]	amābar	amābāris	amābātur	amābāmur	amābāminī	amābantur

ENGLISH	SINGULAR			PLURAL		
	1ST	2ND	3RD	1ST	2ND	3RD
PRESENT	I love	you love	he/she/it loves	we love	you all love	they love
FUTURE	I will love	you will love	he/she/it will love	we will love	you all will love	they will love
IMPERFECT	I was loving	you were loving	he/she/it was loving	we were loving	you all were loving	they were loving
PERFECT	I have loved	you have loved	he/she/it has loved	we have loved	you all have loved	they have loved
FUTURE PERFECT	I will have loved	you will have loved	he/she/it will have loved	we will have loved	you all will have loved	they will have loved
PLUPERFECT	I had loved	you had loved	he/she/it had loved	we had loved	you all had loved	they had loved
PRESENT [PV]	I am loved	you are loved	he/she/it is loved	we are loved	you all are loved	they are loved
FUTURE [PV]	I will be loved	you will be loved	he/she/it will be loved	we will be loved	you all will be loved	they will be loved
IMPERFECT [PV]	I was being loved	you were being loved	he/she/it was being loved	we were being loved	you all were being loved	they were being loved

LATIN	SINGULAR			PLURAL		
	1ST	2ND	3RD	1ST	2ND	3RD
PRESENT	videō	vidēs	videt	vidēmus	vidētis	vident
FUTURE	vidēbō	vidēbis	vidēbit	vidēbimus	vidēbitis	vidēbunt
IMPERFECT	vidēbam	vidēbās	vidēbat	vidēbāmus	vidēbātis	vidēbant
PERFECT	vidī	vidistī	vidit	vidimus	vidistis	vidērunt
FUTURE PERFECT	viderō	videris	viderit	viderimus	videritis	viderint
PLUPERFECT	videram	viderās	viderat	viderāmus	viderātis	viderant
PRESENT [PV]	videor	vidēris	vidētur	vidēmur	vidēminī	videntur
FUTURE [PV]	vidēbor	vidēberis	vidēbitur	vidēbimur	vidēbiminī	vidēbuntur
IMPERFECT [PV]	vidēbar	vidēbāris	vidēbātur	vidēbāmur	vidēbāminī	vidēbantur

ENGLISH	SINGULAR			PLURAL		
	1ST	2ND	3RD	1ST	2ND	3RD
PRESENT	I see	you see	he/she/it sees	we see	you all see	they see
FUTURE	I will see	you will see	he/she/it will see	we will see	you all will see	they will see
IMPERFECT	I was seeing	you were seeing	he/she/it was seeing	we were seeing	you all were seeing	they were seeing
PERFECT	I have seen	you have seen	he/she/it has seen	we have seen	you all have seen	they have seen
FUTURE PERFECT	I will have seen	you will have seen	he/she/it will have seen	we will have seen	you all will have seen	they will have seen
PLUPERFECT	I had seen	you had seen	he/she/it had seen	we had seen	you all had seen	they had seen
PRESENT [PV]	I am seen	you are seen	he/she/it is seen	we are seen	you all are seen	they are seen
FUTURE [PV]	I will be seen	you will be seen	he/she/it will be seen	we will be seen	you all will be seen	they will be seen
IMPERFECT [PV]	I was being seen	you were being seen	he/she/it was being seen	we were being seen	you all were being seen	they were being seen

LATIN	SINGULAR			PLURAL		
	1ST	2ND	3RD	1ST	2ND	3RD
PRESENT	dūcō	dūcis	dūcit	dūcimus	dūcitis	dūcunt
FUTURE	dūcam	dūcēs	dūcet	dūcēmus	dūcētis	dūcent
IMPERFECT	dūcēbam	dūcēbās	dūcēbat	dūcēbāmus	dūcēbātis	dūcēbant
PERFECT	dūxī	dūxistī	dūxit	dūximus	dūxistis	dūxērunt
FUTURE PERFECT	dūxerō	dūxeris	dūxerit	dūxerimus	dūxeritis	dūxerint
PLUPERFECT	dūxeram	dūxerās	dūxerat	dūxerāmus	dūxerātis	viderant
PRESENT [PV]	dūcor	dūcēris	dūcitur	dūcimur	dūciminī	dūcuntur
FUTURE [PV]	dūcar	dūcēris	dūcētur	dūcēmur	dūcēminī	dūcentur
IMPERFECT [PV]	dūcēbar	dūcēbāris	dūcēbātur	dūcēbāmur	dūcēbāminī	dūcēbantur

ENGLISH	SINGULAR			PLURAL		
	1ST	2ND	3RD	1ST	2ND	3RD
PRESENT	I lead	you lead	he/she/it leads	we lead	you all lead	they lead
FUTURE	I will lead	you will lead	he/she/it will lead	we will lead	you all will lead	they will lead
IMPERFECT	I was leading	you were leading	he/she/it was leading	we were leading	you all were leading	they were leading
PERFECT	I have led	you have led	he/she/it has led	we have led	you all have led	they have led
FUTURE PERFECT	I will have led	you will have led	he/she/it will have led	we will have led	you all will have led	they will have led
PLUPERFECT	I had led	you had led	he/she/it had led	we had led	you all had led	they had led
PRESENT [PV]	I am led	you are led	he/she/it is led	we are led	you all are led	they are led
FUTURE [PV]	I will be led	you will be led	he/she/it will be led	we will be led	you all will be led	they will be led
IMPERFECT [PV]	I was being led	you were being led	he/she/it was being led	we were being led	you all were being led	they were being led

GLOSSARY

A

accūsō, accūsāre *I accuse, blame* [1st conj., Wk. 14]

administrō, administrāre *I help, manage* [1st conj., Wk. 14]

adulēscēns, adulēscentis (m) *young man* [3rd decl., Wk. 18]

aedificium, -ī (n) *building* [2nd decl., Wk. 3]

aequus, -a, -um *level, even, calm* [Wk. 6]

aestās, aestātis (f) *summer* [3rd decl., Wk. 29]

aeternus, -a, -um *eternal* [Wk. 11]

agō, agere, *I do, act* [3rd conj., Wk. 12]

agricola, -ae (m) *farmer* [1st decl., Wk. 5]

āla, -ae (f) *wing* [1st decl., Wk. 9]

albus, -a, -um *white* [Wk. 6]

alga, -ae (f) *seaweed* [1st decl., Wk. 6]

aliēnus, -a, -um *foreign* [Wk. 9]

ambulō, ambulāre *I walk* [1st conj., Wk. 3]

amīcus, -ī (m) *friend* [2nd decl., Wk. 1]

amō, amāre, *I love* [1st conj., Wk. 3]

ancora, -ae (f) *anchor* [1st decl., Wk. 9]

antīquus, -a, -um *ancient* [Wk. 10]

appāreō, appārēre *I appear* [2nd conj., Wk. 5]

appellō, appellāre *I name, call, call by, name* [1st conj., Wk. 24]

aprīcus, -a, -um *sunny* [Wk. 2]

aptus, -a, -um *suitable, fit, ready* [Wk. 9]

aqua, -ae (f) *water* [1st decl., Wk. 1]

aquila, -ae (m/f) *eagle* [1st decl., Wk. 5]

aranea, -ae (f) *spider* [1st decl., Wk. 15]

arbor, arboris (f) *tree* [3rd decl., Wk. 26]

architectus, -ī (m) *architect, inventor* [2nd decl., Wk. 22]

arcus, -ūs (m) *bow, arch, rainbow* [4th decl., Wk. 23]

argūmentum, -ī (n) *proof, evidence* [2nd decl., Wk. 16]

āridus, -a, -um *dry* [Wk. 6]

ariēna, -ae (f) *banana* [1st decl., Wk. 2]

ariēs, arietis (m) *ram* [3rd decl., Wk. 13]

armentum, -ī (n) *herd* [2nd decl., Wk. 5]

arō, arāre *I plow* [1st conj., Wk. 14]

asinus, -ī (m) *donkey* [2nd decl., Wk. 21]

astō, astāre *I stand near, stand by* [1st conj., Wk. 1]

astrum, -ī (n) *star, constellation* [2nd decl., Wk. 9]

audeō, audēre *I dare* [2nd conj., Wk. 8]

augeō, augēre *I increase* [2nd conj., Wk. 7]

aurōra, -ae (f) *dawn* [1st decl., Wk. 9]

avārus, -a, -um *greedy* [Wk. 27]

avia, -ae (f) *grandmother* [1st decl., Wk. 12]

avus, -ī (m) *grandfather* [2nd decl., Wk. 12]

B

bālaena, -ae (f) *whale* [1st decl., Wk. 6]

balatrō, balatrōnis (m) *jester, clown* [3rd decl., Wk. 13]

beātus, -a, -um, *happy, blessed* [Wk. 10]

bestiola, -ae (f) *insect* [1st decl., Wk. 15]

bibō, bibere, *I drink* [3rd conj., Wk. 30]

bonus, -a, -um, *good* [Wk. 11]

bōs, bovis (m/f) *ox, bull, cow* [3rd decl., Wk. 18]

Brittania, -ae (f) *Britain* [1st decl., Wk. 31]

brūnus, -a, -um, *brown* [Wk. 4]

būtūrum, -ī (n) *butter* [2nd decl., Wk. 30]

C

cadō, cadere *I fall, sink, drop* [3rd conj., Wk. 26]
caecus, -a, -um *blind* [Wk. 11]
caelum, -ī (n) *sky, heaven* [2nd decl., Wk. 1]
caeruleus, -a, -um *blue* [Wk. 15]
caldus, -a, -um *warm, hot, fiery* [Wk. 23]
camēlus, -ī (m) *camel* [2nd decl., Wk. 28]
candēla, -ae (f) *candle* [1st decl., Wk. 20]
cantō, cantāre *I sing, play (music)* [1st conj., Wk. 20]
cantus, -ūs (m) *song, singing* [4th decl., Wk. 24]
caper, caprī (m) *billy goat* [2nd decl., Wk. 13]
captīvus, -ī (m) *captive* [2nd decl., Wk. 17]
captō, captāre *I hunt* [1st conj., Wk. 22]
caput, capitis (n) *head* [3rd decl., Wk. 15]
carcer, carceris (m) *prison* [3rd decl., Wk. 27]
carmen, carminis (n) *song, poem* [3rd decl., Wk. 20]
carō, carnis (f) *meat, flesh* [3rd decl., Wk. 28]
Carthāgō, Carthāginis (f) *Carthage* [3rd decl., Wk. 29]
cauda, -ae (f) *tail* [1st decl., Wk. 13]
cavea, -ae (f) *cage, animal den* [1st decl., Wk. 13]
caveō, cavēre *I guard against, beware* [2nd conj., Wk. 27]
celsus, -a, -um *tall, high, lofty* [Wk. 29]
cēna, -ae (f) *dinner, meal* [1st decl., Wk. 3]
censeō, censēre *I estimate* [2nd conj., Wk. 7]
centaurus, -ī (m) *centaur* [2nd decl., Wk. 22]
certātim, *eagerly* [Wk. 12]
cervus, -ī (m) *stag, deer* [2nd decl., Wk. 5]
cibō, cibāre *I feed* [1st conj., Wk. 7]
cibus, -ī (m) *food* [2nd decl., Wk. 1]
circus, -ī (m) *circle, racecourse* [2nd decl., Wk. 13]
clam, *secretly* [Wk. 23]
clāmō, clāmāre *I shout* [1st conj., Wk. 5]
cōgitō, cōgitāre *I think* [1st conj., Wk. 11]
colōnus, -ī (m) *settler* [2nd decl., Wk. 1]
coma, -ae (f) *hair, leaves, wool, mane* [1st decl., Wk. 5]
commemorō, commemorāre *I remember, mention, call to mind* [1st conj., Wk. 17]
commendō, commendāre *I commit, entrust* [1st conj., Wk. 24]
commūnicō, commūnicāre *I share, inform* [1st conj., Wk. 22]
consecō, consecāre *I chop, cut up* [1st conj., Wk. 30]
contentus, -a, -um *satisfied, content* [Wk. 16]
coquō, coquere *I cook, bake* [3rd conj., Wk. 30]
coquus, -ī (m) *cook, chef* [2nd decl., Wk. 4]
cor, cordis (n) *heart* [3rd decl., Wk. 20]
cornix, cornicis (f) *crow* [3rd decl., Wk. 15]
cornū, -ūs (n) *horn* [4th decl., Wk. 25]
corpus, corporis (n) *body* [3rd decl., Wk. 15]
crās, *tomorrow* [Wk. 12]
crēdō, crēdere *I believe* [2nd conj., Wk. 24]
crescō, crescere *I grow, arise* [3rd conj., Wk. 10]
crūs, crūris (n) *leg* [3rd decl., Wk. 15]
crūstulum, -ī (n) *cookie, small cake* [2nd decl., Wk. 30]
crux, crucis (f) *cross* [3rd decl., Wk. 21]
culter, -trī (m) *knife* [2nd decl., Wk. 25]
cumulō, cumulāre *I pile up, fill up* [1st conj., Wk. 4]
cunīculus, -ī (m) *rabbit* [2nd decl., Wk. 2]
cūrō, cūrāre *I care for* [1st conj., Wk. 25]
currō, currere *I run* [3rd conj., Wk. 13]
cyclops, cyclōpis (m) *cyclops* [3rd decl., Wk. 22]
cȳgnus, -ī (m) *swan* [2nd decl., Wk. 28]

D

dēbeō, dēbēre *I owe, ought* [2nd conj., Wk. 27]

dēclārō, dēclārāre *I declare, explain* [1st conj., Wk. 11]

dēliciōsus, -a, -um *delicious* [Wk. 2]

delphīnus, -ī (m) *dolphin* [2nd decl., Wk. 6]

dēmōnstrō, dēmōnstrāre *I show* [1st conj., Wk. 19]

Deus, -ī (m) *God* [2nd decl., Wk. 11]

dīrigō, dīrigere *I direct* [3rd conj., Wk. 32]

disciplīna, -ae (f) *instruction, training* [1st decl., Wk. 17]

discipulus, -ī (m) *apprentice, student* [2nd decl., Wk. 16]

dō, dāre *I give* [1st conj., Wk. 18]

dominus, -ī (m) *lord, master* [2nd decl., Wk. 3]

domō, domāre *I tame, subdue* [1st conj., Wk. 28]

domus, -ūs (f) *home, house* [4th decl., Wk. 24]

dracō, dracōnis (m) *dragon* [3rd decl., Wk. 22]

dubitō, dubitāre *I doubt, hesitate* [1st conj., Wk. 14]

dūcō, dūcere *I lead* [3rd conj., Wk. 9]

dux, ducis (m) *leader* [3rd decl., Wk. 21]

E

edō, edere *I eat* [3rd conj., Wk. 18]

ēgregius, -a, -um *outstanding* [Wk. 27]

elephantus, -ī (m) *elephant* [2nd decl., Wk. 13]

emō, emere *I buy, purchase* [3rd conj., Wk. 30]

epistula, -ae (f) *letter* [1st decl., Wk. 3]

eques, equitis (m) *horseman, knight* [3rd decl., Wk. 31]

equitō, equitāre *I ride (horseback)* [1st conj., Wk. 31]

equus, -ī (m) *horse* [2nd decl., Wk. 1]

eram, *I was* [Wk. 30]

erō, *I will be* [Wk. 16]

errō, errāre *I wander* [1st conj., Wk. 5]

et, *and* [Wk. 6]

Eurōpa, -ae (f) *Europe* [1st decl., Wk. 29]

exanimō, exanimāre *I kill* [1st conj., Wk. 7]

exerceō, exercēre *I train, exercise* [2nd conj., Wk. 19]

exercitus, -ūs (m) *army* [4th decl., Wk. 31]

explōrō, explōrāre *I find out, explore* [1st conj., Wk. 14]

exspectō, exspectāre *I wait, wait for, expect* [1st conj., Wk. 23]

exsultō, exsultāre *I leap up, dance, rejoice* [1st conj., Wk. 3]

extrēmus, -a, -um *last, farthest, outermost* [Wk. 31]

F

fābula, -ae (f) *story, legend* [1st decl., Wk. 3]

famēlicus, -a, -um *hungry* [Wk. 10]

familia, -ae (f) *family, household* [1st decl., Wk. 11]

farīna, -ae (f) *flour* [1st decl., Wk. 30]

fēmina, -ae (f) *woman* [1st decl., Wk. 3]

ferus, -ī (m) *wild animal* [2nd decl., Wk. 17]

fessus, -a, -um *tired, weary* [Wk. 18]

fīdus, -a, -um *faithful, trustworthy* [Wk. 24]

fīgō, fīgere *I fasten, attach, make firm* [3rd conj., Wk. 15]

fīlia, -ae (f) *daughter* [1st decl., Wk. 3]

fīlius, -ī (m) *son* [2nd decl., Wk. 3]

fīlum, -ī (n) *thread, string* [2nd decl., Wk. 22]

fīnitimus, -ī (m) *neighbor* [2nd decl., Wk. 29]

firmus, -a, -um *strong, firm, steadfast* [Wk. 16]

flagellum, -ī (n) *whip* [2nd decl., Wk. 13]

flagrō, flagrāre *I blaze, flame, burn* [1st conj., Wk. 26]

flavus, -a, -um *yellow, blond* [Wk. 15]
fleō, flēre *I weep* [2nd conj., Wk. 16]
flō, flāre *I blow, breathe* [1st conj., Wk. 11]
flōreō, flōrēre *I flourish* [2nd conj., Wk. 21]
flōs, flōris (m) *flower* [3rd decl., Wk. 20]
flūmen, flūminis (n) *river* [3rd decl., Wk. 17]
fluvius, -ī (m) *river, stream* [2nd decl., Wk. 9]
foedus, -a, -um *horrible, ugly* [Wk. 10]
folium, -ī (n) *leaf* [2nd decl., Wk. 2]
forum, -ī (n) *public square, marketplace* [2nd decl., Wk. 3]
foveō, fovēre *I cherish, love, esteem* [2nd conj., Wk. 23]
frāgum, -ī (n) *strawberry* [2nd decl., Wk. 2]
frangō, frangere *I break* [3rd conj., Wk. 30]
frāter, frātris (m) *brother* [3rd decl., Wk. 24]
frūctus, -ūs (m) *fruit, profit* [4th decl., Wk. 23]
fulmen, fulmenis (n) *lightning, thunderbolt* [3rd decl., Wk. 26]
fungus, -ī (m) *mushroom, fungus* [2nd decl., Wk. 4]
fuscina, -ae (f) *harpoon, trident* [1st decl., Wk. 6]

G

Gallia, -ae (f) *Gaul* [1st decl., Wk. 29]
gaudeō, gaudēre *I rejoice* [2nd conj., Wk. 11]
gelidus, -a, -um *cold, icy* [Wk. 9]
gelū, -ūs (n) *chill, frost* [4th decl., Wk. 25]
genū, -ūs (n) *knee* [4th decl., Wk. 25]
germāna, -ae (f) *sister* [1st decl., Wk. 11]
Germānia, -ae (f) *Germany* [1st decl., Wk. 31]
germānus, -ī (m) *brother* [2nd decl., Wk. 11]
gigās, gigantis (m) *giant* [3rd decl., Wk. 22]
grex, gregis (m) *flock, herd* [3rd decl., Wk. 25]
grȳps, grȳphis (m) *griffin* [3rd decl., Wk. 22]
gustō, gustāre *I taste* [1st conj., Wk. 2]

H

habēna, -ae (f) *strap, rein* [1st decl., Wk. 17]
habeō, habēre *I have, hold* [2nd conj., Wk. 20]
habitō, habitāre *I live in, dwell, inhabit* [1st conj., Wk. 31]
harēna, -ae (f) *sand* [1st decl., Wk. 6]
hasta, -ae (f) *spear, lance* [1st decl., Wk. 19]
herba, -ae (f) *herb, grass* [1st decl., Wk. 28]
herī, *yesterday* [Wk. 12]
hiemō, hiemāre *I spend the winter* [1st conj., Wk. 9]
hiems, hiemis (f) *winter, bad weather* [3rd decl., Wk. 29]
hippopotāmus, -ī (m) *hippopotamus* [2nd decl., Wk. 28]
Hispānia, -ae (f) *Spain* [1st decl., Wk. 31]
hodiē, *today* [Wk. 12]
homō, hominis (m) *man, human being* [3rd decl., Wk. 29]
honestus, -a, -um *honorable* [Wk. 14]
hortus, -ī (m) *garden* [2nd decl., Wk. 2]
hyaena, -ae (f) *hyena* [1st decl., Wk. 28]
hydrus, -ī (m) *sea serpent* [2nd decl., Wk. 6]

I

iaceō, iacēre *I lie down* [2nd conj., Wk. 27]
Iesus, -ūs (m) *Jesus* [4th decl., Wk. 24]
imber, imbris (m) *rain* [3rd decl., Wk. 26]
imperō, imperāre *I order* [1st conj., Wk. 21]
improbus, -a, -um *wicked* [Wk. 14]
incendō, incendere *I kindle, set on fire* [3rd conj., Wk. 26]

inimīcus, -ī (m) *personal enemy* [2nd decl., Wk. 7]

insidiae, -ārum (f) *ambush, trap, plot* [1st decl., Wk. 14]

instō, instāre *I pursue eagerly, follow closely* [1st conj., Wk. 6]

īnsula, -ae (f) *island* [1st decl., Wk. 17]

intrō, intrāre, *I enter* [1st conj., Wk. 14]

Ītalia, -ae (f) *Italy* [1st decl., Wk. 29]

iter, itineris (n) *journey* [3rd decl., Wk. 21]

iūdicō, iūdicāre *I judge* [1st conj., Wk. 11]

iungō, iungere *I join, unite, yoke* [3rd conj., Wk. 18]

iūs, iūris (n) *justice, right, law* [3rd decl., Wk. 16]

iūstus, -a, -um *just, righteous* [Wk. 11]

L

labor, labōris (m) *work, labor* [3rd decl., Wk. 18]

labōrō, labōrāre *I work, toil* [1st conj., Wk. 5]

labyrinthus, -ī (m) *labyrinth, maze* [2nd decl., Wk. 22]

lāc, lactis (n) *milk* [3rd decl., Wk. 30]

lacrima, -ae (f) *tear* [1st decl., Wk. 16]

lacus, -ūs (m) *lake, tub, hollow* [4th decl., Wk. 23]

laetus, -a, -um *happy, joyful* [Wk. 11]

latebra, -ae (f) *hiding place* [1st decl., Wk. 1]

latrō, latrōnis (m) *robber* [3rd decl., Wk. 27]

lātus, -a, -um *wide, broad* [Wk. 9]

latus, lateris (n) *flank, side* [3rd decl., Wk. 18]

laudō, laudāre *I praise* [1st conj., Wk. 3]

laxō, laxāre *I loosen* [1st conj., Wk. 17]

lēgātus, -ī (m) *lieutenant* [2nd decl., Wk. 17]

leō, leōnis (m) *lion* [3rd decl., Wk. 25]

lēx, lēgis (f) *law* [3rd decl., Wk. 27]

liber, librī (m) *book* [2nd decl., Wk. 11]

līberō, līberāre *I set free* [1st conj., Wk. 14]

lībō, lībāre *I sip, taste* [1st conj., Wk. 5]

lignum, -ī (n) *wood, timber* [2nd decl., Wk. 26]

lingua, -ae (f) *tongue, language* [1st decl., Wk. 3]

littera, -ae (f) *letter of the alphabet,* PLURAL: *letter, epistle* [1st decl., Wk. 12]

longinquus, -a, -um *far away, distant* [Wk. 31]

lūceō, lūcēre *I shine, am bright* [2nd conj., Wk. 5]

lūdō, lūdere *I play, tease, trick* [3rd conj., Wk. 20]

lūgeō, lūgēre *I grieve, mourn* [2nd conj., Wk. 11]

lūna, -ae (f) *moon* [1st decl., Wk. 5]

lupus, -ī (m) *wolf* [2nd decl., Wk. 5]

lutum, -ī (n) *mud* [2nd decl., Wk. 26]

lux, lūcis (f) *light* [3rd decl., Wk. 20]

luxuria, -ae (f) *luxury, extravagance* [1st decl., Wk. 19]

lyra, -ae (f) *lyre* [1st decl., Wk. 20]

M

maculōsus, -a, -um *spotted, stained* [Wk. 10]

magister, magistrī (m) *teacher (male)* [2nd decl., Wk. 16]

magistra, -ae (f) *teacher (female)* [1st decl., Wk. 16]

magnus, -a, -um *large, big* [Wk. 2]

mālum, -ī (n) *apple* [2nd decl., Wk. 2]

malus, -a, -um *bad, evil* [Wk. 2]

maneō, manēre *I remain, stay* [2nd conj., Wk. 8]

mannus, -ī (m) *pony* [2nd decl., Wk. 13]

manus, -ūs (f) *hand* [4th decl., Wk. 24]

māter, mātris (f) *mother* [3rd decl., Wk. 24]

matrimonium, -ī (n) *marriage* [2nd decl., Wk. 12]

memoria, -ae (f) *memory* [1st decl., Wk. 17]

mensa, -ae (f) *table* [1st decl., Wk. 3]

mereō, merēre *I deserve, earn, am worthy of* [2nd conj., Wk. 27]

metus, -ūs (m) *fear, dread* [4th decl., Wk. 24]
mīles, mīlitis (m) *soldier* [3rd decl., Wk. 27]
mīnōtaurus, -ī (m) *minotaur* [2nd decl., Wk. 22]
minūtātim, *gradually, bit by bit* [Wk. 12]
mīrus, -a, -um *strange, wonderful* [Wk. 9]
mittō, mittere *I send, let go* [3rd conj., Wk. 15]
moenia, -ium (n, pl) *fortifications, city walls* [2nd decl., Wk. 21]
moneō, monēre *I warn* [2nd conj., Wk. 16]
morbus, -ī (m) *sickness, disease* [2nd decl., Wk. 7]
mordeō, mordēre *I bite, sting* [2nd conj., Wk. 28]
moveō, movēre *I move* [2nd conj., Wk. 21]
mox, *soon* [Wk. 26]
mūnicipium, -ī (n) *free town* [2nd decl., Wk. 19]
mūnus, mūneris (n) *duty, office* [3rd decl., Wk. 27]
mūrus, -ī (m) *wall* [2nd decl., Wk. 1]
musca, -ae (f) *fly* [1st decl., Wk. 15]
mūtō, mūtāre *I change* [1st conj., Wk. 11]

N

narrō, narrāre *I tell, relate, recount* [1st conj., Wk. 14]
nasus, -ī (m) *nose* [2nd decl., Wk. 4]
nausea, -ae (f) *nausea, seasickness* [1st decl., Wk. 6]
nauta, -ae (m) *sailor* [1st decl., Wk. 1]
nāvigō, nāvigāre *I sail* [1st conj., Wk. 9]
nimbus, -ī (m) *thundercloud, storm* [2nd decl., Wk. 1]
nix, nivis (f) *snow* [3rd decl., Wk. 23]
nō, nāre, *I swim* [1st conj., Wk. 22]
noctua, -ae (f) *owl* [1st decl., Wk. 8]
nōmen, nōminis (n) *name* [3rd decl., Wk. 21]
nōn, *not* [Wk. 12]
novus, -a, -um *new* [Wk. 23]

nūbēs, nūbis (f) *cloud, gloom* [3rd decl., Wk. 26]
nucleus, -ī (m) *nut, kernel* [2nd decl., Wk. 4]
numquam, *never* [Wk. 28]
nuntiō, nuntiāre *I announce, declare* [1st conj., Wk. 14]
nuntius, -ī (m) *message, messenger* [2nd decl., Wk. 5]

O

obsecrō, obsecrāre *I beg, implore* [1st conj., Wk. 14]
obsideō, obsidēre *I remain near, besiege* [2nd conj., Wk. 19]
occultō, occultāre *I hide, conceal* [1st conj., Wk. 3]
occupō, occupāre *I seize* [1st conj., Wk. 8]
ōceanus, -ī (m) *ocean* [2nd decl., Wk. 6]
odōrātus, -a, -um *sweet-smelling, fragrant* [Wk. 4]
olefactō, olefactāre *I smell, sniff* [1st conj., Wk. 4]
opācus, -a, -um *dark, shaded* [Wk. 23]
opera, -ae (f) *effort, services* [1st decl., Wk. 7]
oppidum, -ī (n) *town* [2nd decl., Wk. 19]
oppugnō, oppugnāre *I attack* [1st conj., Wk. 7]
ornō, ornāre *I equip, decorate* [1st conj., Wk. 17]
ōs, ōris (n) *mouth* [3rd decl., Wk. 18]
ōvum, -ī (n) *egg* [2nd decl., Wk. 30]

P

pābulum, -ī (n) *fodder, food for animals* [2nd decl., Wk. 13]
pacō, pacāre *I pacify, subdue* [1st conj., Wk. 19]
palma, -ae (f) *palm of the hand, palm tree* [1st decl., Wk. 21]
pardus, -ī (m) *panther, leopard* [2nd decl., Wk. 28]
pāreō, pārēre *I obey* [2nd conj., Wk. 13]
parō, parāre *I prepare* [1st conj., Wk. 7]

parvus, -a, -um *little, small* [Wk. 2]
pastor, pastōris (m) *shepherd* [3rd decl., Wk. 25]
patella, -ae (f) *plate, dish* [1st decl., Wk. 30]
pater, patris (m) *father* [3rd decl., Wk. 24]
patria, -ae (f) *native land* [1st decl., Wk. 17]
pax, pācis (f) *peace* [3rd decl., Wk. 16]
peccō, peccāre *I sin* [1st conj., Wk. 1]
pecū, -ūs (n) *cattle, flock* [4th decl., Wk. 25]
pecūnia, -ae (f) *money* [1st decl., Wk. 27]
pēgasus, -ī (m) *pegasus* [2nd decl., Wk. 22]
perfectus, -a, um *perfect* [Wk. 4]
pēs, pedis (m) *foot* [3rd decl., Wk. 18]
pharetra, -ae (f) *quiver* [1st decl., Wk. 7]
pinna, -ae *(f) feather, wing* [1st decl., Wk. 15]
pirum, -ī (n) *pear* [2nd decl., Wk. 2]
pōculum, -ī (n) *cup* [2nd decl., Wk. 30]
poēta, -ae (m) *poet* [1st decl., Wk. 1]
pōnō, pōnere *I put, place* [3rd conj., Wk. 32]
pontus, -ī (m) *sea, seawater* [2nd decl., Wk. 1]
porcus, -ī (m) *pig* [2nd decl., Wk. 4]
porta, -ae (f) *door, gate* [1st decl., Wk. 3]
portō, portāre *I carry* [1st conj., Wk. 20]
portus, -ūs (m) *port, harbor* [4th decl., Wk. 23]
possum, posse *I am able* [Wk. 27]
praedīcō, pradīcere *I proclaim* [3rd conj., Wk. 32]
princeps, principis (n) *chief* [3rd decl., Wk. 21]
probō, probāre *I approve* [1st conj., Wk. 3]
properō, properāre *I hurry, rush* [1st conj., Wk. 5]
prōra, -ae (f) *prow (of a ship)* [1st decl., Wk. 9]
prōvincia, -ae (f) *province* [1st decl., Wk. 19]
psittācus, -ī (m) *parrot* [2nd decl., Wk. 28]
puella, -ae (f) *girl* [1st decl., Wk. 1]
puer, puerī (m) *boy* [2nd decl., Wk. 1]

pugnō, pugnāre *I fight* [1st conj., Wk. 7]
pulcher, -chra, -chrum *beautiful* [Wk. 10]
pulvereus, -a, -um *dusty, full of dust* [Wk. 18]
pulvīnus, -ī (m) *pillow, cushion* [2nd decl., Wk. 10]
pulvis, pulveris (m) *dirt, dust, powder* [3rd decl., Wk. 18]
pūrpureus, -a, -um *purple* [Wk. 10]
pūrus, -a, -um *pure, clean* [Wk. 10]

Q

quaerō, quaerere *I search for, seek* [3rd conj., Wk. 27]
querēla, -ae (f) *complaint, whining* [1st decl., Wk. 19]
quiescō, quiescere *I rest, sleep* [3rd conj., Wk. 18]
quiētus, -a, -um *quiet, sleeping* [Wk. 10]
quondam, *once, formerly* [Wk. 31]

R

radius, -ī (m) *staff, rod* [2nd decl., Wk. 4]
rādix, rādīcis (f) *root* [3rd decl., Wk. 26]
rāmus, -ī (m) *branch, twig* [2nd decl., Wk. 26]
recuperō, recuperāre *I recover* [1st conj., Wk. 14]
rēgīna, -ae (f) *queen* [1st decl., Wk. 14]
regnō, regnāre *I rule, govern, reign* [1st conj., Wk. 14]
regnum, -ī (n) *kingdom* [2nd decl., Wk. 31]
removeō, removēre *I remove, take away* [2nd conj., Wk. 19]
rēmus, -ī (m) *oar* [2nd decl., Wk. 9]
repente, *suddenly* [Wk. 24]
reptō, reptāre *I crawl, creep* [1st conj., Wk. 15]
repudiō, repudiāre *I reject, scorn* [1st conj., Wk. 16]

respondeō, respondēre *I respond, answer* [2nd conj., Wk. 16]

retineō, retinēre *I hold back, retain* [2nd conj., Wk. 17]

rēx, rēgis (m) *king* [3rd decl., Wk. 14]

rhīnocerōs, rhīnocerōtis (m) *rhinoceros* [3rd decl., Wk. 28]

rīdeō, rīdēre *I laugh* [2nd conj., Wk. 6]

rīdiculus, -a, -um *funny, amusing* [Wk. 10]

rīpa, -ae (f) *riverbank* [1st decl., Wk. 5]

rogō, rogāre, *I ask* [1st conj., Wk. 14]

Rōma, -ae (f) *Rome* [1st decl., Wk. 29]

ruber, -bra, -brum *red* [Wk. 22]

rudō, rudere *I roar, bellow, bray* [3rd conj., Wk. 13]

S

sacchārum, -ī (n) *sugar* [2nd decl., Wk. 30]

sagitta, -ae (f) *arrow* [1st decl., Wk. 7]

salsus, -a, -um *salty, witty* [Wk. 6]

satis, *enough* [Wk. 12]

satyrus, -ī (m) *satyr, faun* [2nd decl., Wk. 22]

saxum, -ī (n) *rock* [2nd decl., Wk. 5]

scalpō, scalpere *I carve, scratch* [3rd conj., Wk. 15]

sciūrus, -ī (m) *squirrel* [2nd decl., Wk. 8]

scrībō, scrībere *I write* [3rd conj., Wk. 12]

sedeō, sedēre *I sit* [2nd conj., Wk. 16]

sella, -ae (f) *seat, chair* [1st decl., Wk. 3]

sēmen, sēminis (n) *seed* [3rd decl., Wk. 18]

semper, *always* [Wk. 12]

sepulcrum, -ī (n) *tomb, grave* [2nd decl., Wk. 27]

serēnus, -a, -um *calm, bright, clear* [Wk. 9]

serō, serere *I sow, plant* [3rd conj., Wk. 12]

serpēns, serpentis (m/f) *serpent, snake* [3rd decl., Wk. 28]

servō, servāre *I save* [1st conj., Wk. 17]

servus, -ī (m) *slave, servant* [2nd decl., Wk. 14]

significō, significāre *I indicate, point out* [1st conj., Wk. 7]

silva, -ae (f) *forest* [1st decl., Wk. 4]

sīmia, -ae (f) *ape, monkey* [1st decl., Wk. 28]

simul, *at the same time* [Wk. 12]

sīve, *or* [Wk. 30]

sōl, sōlis (m) *sun* [3rd decl., Wk. 23]

somniō, somniāre *I dream* [1st conj., Wk. 10]

somnus, -ī (m) *sleep* [2nd decl., Wk. 10]

soror, sorōris (f) *sister* [3rd decl., Wk. 24]

spectō, spectāre *I look at, watch* [1st conj., Wk. 9]

spērō, spērāre *I hope* [1st conj., Wk. 11]

spīritus, -ūs (m) *spirit, breath* [4th decl., Wk. 24]

spīrō, spīrāre *I breathe* [1st conj., Wk. 5]

stabulum, -ī (n) *stall, stable* [2nd decl., Wk. 19]

statim, *immediately* [Wk. 6]

stella, -ae (f) *star* [1st decl., Wk. 1]

stimulus, -ī (m) *goad, spur* [2nd decl., Wk. 17]

sub, *below, under* [Wk. 4]

sum, *I am* [Wk. 10]

superō, superāre *I defeat, conquer* [1st conj., Wk. 7]

suprā, *above* [Wk. 4]

T

tangō, tangere *I touch, strike* [3rd conj., Wk. 26]

tardus, -a, -um *slow* [Wk. 10]

taurus, -ī (m) *bull* [2nd decl., Wk. 1]

tectum, -ī (n) *roof, ceiling, dwelling* [2nd decl., Wk. 19]

tellūs, tellūris (f) *earth, ground, land* [3rd decl., Wk. 23]

tempestās, tempestātis (f) *weather, storm* [3rd decl., Wk. 25]

tempus, temporis (n) *time* [3rd decl., Wk. 20]

terminus, -ī (m) *end, boundary, limit* [2nd decl., Wk. 29]

terra, -ae (f) *earth, land* [1st decl., Wk. 1]

terreō, terrēre *I frighten, terrify* [2nd conj., Wk. 25]

tībia, -ae (f) *flute, pipe* [1st decl., Wk. 21]

tigris, tigridis (m/f) *tiger* [3rd decl., Wk. 13]

timeō, timēre *I fear* [2nd conj., Wk. 16]

tondeō, tondēre *I clip, give a haircut, shear* [2nd conj., Wk. 25]

tonitrus, -ūs (m) *thunder* [4th decl., Wk. 26]

trochus, -ī (m) *hoop for games* [2nd decl., Wk. 13]

tuba, -ae (f) *trumpet* [1st decl., Wk. 31]

turba, -ae (f) *crowd, mob* [1st decl., Wk. 3]

tūtus, -a, -um *safe, secure* [Wk. 25]

U

ulmus, -ī (m) *elm tree* [2nd decl., Wk. 4]

ululō, ululāre *I howl, scream* [1st conj., Wk. 5]

umbra, -ae (f) *shadow, shade* [1st decl., Wk. 23]

ūmidus, -a, -um *wet* [Wk. 6]

ūnā, *together, in one* [Wk. 18]

unda, -ae (f) *wave* [1st decl., Wk. 9]

undique, *on/from all sides, from every direction* [Wk. 29]

ursa, -ae (f) *or* **ursus,** -ī (m) *bear* [1st decl. or 2nd decl., Wk. 28]

ūva, -ae (f) *grape* [1st decl., Wk. 2]

V

vadum, -ī (n) *ford, shallows* [2nd decl., Wk. 31]

valeō, valēre *I am well* [2nd conj., Wk. 8]

vastō, vastāre *I devastate, lay waste* [1st conj., Wk. 26]

vehō, vehere *I carry, ride, convey* [3rd conj., Wk. 21]

vēlum, -ī (n) *sail, curtain* [2nd decl., Wk. 9]

venēnum, -ī (n) *poison* [2nd decl., Wk. 7]

ventus, -ī (m) *wind* [2nd decl., Wk. 7]

verbum, -ī (n) *word* [2nd decl., Wk. 11]

verū, -ūs (n) *javelin, spit (for roasting meat)* [4th decl., Wk. 25]

vesper, vesperis (m) *evening, evening star* [3rd decl., Wk. 20]

vestīmentum, -ī (n) *clothing, garment* [2nd decl., Wk. 21]

vexō, vexāre *I annoy, harass* [1st conj., Wk. 29]

vibrō, vibrāre *I wave, shake* [1st conj., Wk. 21]

victōria, -ae (f) *victory* [1st decl., Wk. 19]

vīcus, -ī (m) *village* [2nd decl., Wk. 23]

videō, vidēre *I see* [2nd conj., Wk. 16]

vigilō, vigilāre *I guard, watch over* [1st conj., Wk. 25]

villa, -ae (f) *farmhouse, country house* [1st decl., Wk. 17]

vincō, vincere *I conquer* [3rd conj., Wk. 32]

vir, virī (m) *man* [2nd decl., Wk. 11]

virga, -ae (f) *branch, twig* [1st decl., Wk. 1]

virgō, virginis (f) *maiden* [3rd decl., Wk. 20]

vītō, vītāre *I avoid* [1st conj., Wk. 29]

vīvō, vīvere *I live* [3rd conj., Wk. 12]

vocō, vocāre *I call, summon, invite* [1st conj., Wk. 14]

volō, volāre *I fly* [1st conj., Wk. 5]

vox, vōcis (f) *voice* [3rd decl., Wk. 20]

vulnerō, vulnerāre *I wound* [1st conj., Wk. 19]

vulnus, vulneris (n) *wound* [3rd decl., Wk. 15]

SOURCES AND HELPS

Brunel Jr., Donald J. *Basic Latin Vocabulary.* Oxford: American Classical League, 1989. In the later stages of developing the curriculum, this was my basic source for choosing and defining vocabulary.

Buehner, William J. and John W. Ambrose. *Introduction to Preparatory Latin,* Book I, 2nd ed. Wellesley Hills: Independent School Press, 1977.

Ehrlich, Eugene. *Amo, Amas, Amat, and More.* New York: Harper and Row, 1985.

Greenough, J. B., J. H. Allen, et al., *Allen & Greenough's New Latin Grammar.* Boston: Ginn and Co., 1903.

Morris, William, ed. *American Heritage Dictionary of the English Language,* New College Edition. Boston: Houghton Mifflin, 1976. This was my basic reference English dictionary and one I would recommend for the teaching of Latin. My main use for it was to confirm and define derivatives.

Schaeffer, Rudolph F. *Latin English Derivative Dictionary,* edited by W. C. Carr. Oxford: American Classical League, 1960.

Simpson, D. P. *Cassell's Latin and English Dictionary.* New York: Macmillan Publishing, 1987. This is my most commonly used Latin dictionary, as well as the one the students used in their work.

Weber, Robertus, ed. *Biblia Sacra Vulgata.* Stuttgart: Wurttembergische Bibelanstalt, 1975. I used this and perhaps other versions for Scripture quotations.

Wheelock, Frederic M. *Latin: An Introductory Course Based on Ancient Authors,* 6th ed. revised. New York: Harper and Row, 2005. I depended upon this for Latin grammar, and I would recommend it for Latin teachers who need more of a Latin background.